Gregg Lewis

original screenplay
by Jam...

World Wide Publications
A ministry of the Billy Graham Evangelistic Association
1303 Hennepin Avenue, Minneapolis, MN 55403

CAUGHT

Copyright, © 1987, World Wide Publications.
Published by World Wide Publications,
1303 Hennepin Avenue,
Minneapolis, Minnesota 55403.

World Wide Publications is the book publishing division of the
Billy Graham Evangelistic Association.

ISBN 0-89066-091-3

Printed in the United States of America

Gregg Lewis is Editor-at-Large for Campus Life *and Senior
Editor for* Partnership. *He has written over 300 articles and
has authored seven books, the most recent of which,* Am I
Alive?, *was a Literary Guild Book Club Selection. He lives
with his wife and four young children in Carol Stream, Illinois.*

CHAPTER 1

A gray morning mist draping down from a colorless sky swirled and mingled with a blanket of fog rising from the rivers and canals of the still slumbering city of Amsterdam. Not many citizens saw the bright yellow jeep zigzagging its way through deserted streets and over ancient bridges. Fewer still gave it or its four occupants a second thought as it left the old central city and headed south through a warehouse district along the Amstel River. And when it rolled to a halt in front of a four-story brick shell in the middle of an entire block of condemned buildings, there were absolutely no witnesses to be seen. Or to see.

The driver jumped out of the jeep first, hurried around the front of the vehicle, and took the arm of a woman sitting in the front passenger seat, pulling as much as helping her out of the jeep. Maintaining his firm hold, he guided the woman toward an open doorway in the boarded-up, brown brick building, as the two backseat passengers climbed out of the jeep. The first, an 18-year-old guy, moving with obvious uncertainty, slowly followed the others into the building. The last man, balancing a still steaming cup of coffee on a saucer, stopped and took a sip. Then he glanced up and down the empty street before he, too, entered the building.

Tim Devon took several steps into the darkness and then had to stop for a minute to let his eyes adjust to the lack of light. When he could make out the figures of Sprug and the woman receding down a hallway to his right, he began to follow, feeling his way around broken boards and over piles of crumbled plaster. He passed the doorway of a room where just enough daylight filtered in around a boarded window for him to see a pile of empty beer cans and some blood-red graffiti—Dutch words he couldn't read.

Whenever he stopped shuffling through the debris, Tim could hear the scratching, skittering sound of rats running away toward the deeper darkness farther into the building. But apart from the rodents, the place was deserted. Even the krakers, bands of squatters who illegally occupied and set up housekeeping in old, abandoned buildings all over Amsterdam, had given up on this place long ago. Although, Tim judged by the odor, the last human occupants hadn't moved out until long after the sewer and water had been disconnected.

Ahead in the darkness, Sprug and the woman disappeared through a passageway to the left. When Tim reached that point, he found a short hallway leading to an even darker stairwell. At first Tim navigated up the stairs mostly by sound, following the noise of footsteps and the voice of Sprug, who was urging the woman along: "Just a little farther, Moira. We've got what you need upstairs."

Beyond the first couple of landings, the way became gradually lighter, presumably from an opening at the top of the stairs. After the unknown blackness at the bottom of the stairwell, daylight should have been reassuring to Tim. But it wasn't.

Following Sprug up to the roof of a deserted building, for

whatever reason, wasn't an appealing idea. Tim didn't know what Sprug had in mind, and he refused to think about the possibilities. But then Tim didn't want to be there at all. What he wanted was to turn and bolt down the stairs. But he could hear Jacques below now, starting up. And Jacques was the one who'd asked him to come along. "I have something I'd like you to see. Something you need to understand," he'd said. The words had been posed as a request. But the tight, cold smile that accompanied the words, and the even colder eyes, had left Tim no choice.

Sprug and Moira had reached the top of the stairs, where a door hung ajar on a single rusty hinge. One kick from Sprug and the door broke away with a crash that echoed down and back up the stairwell. And Tim had to squint against the sudden glare of the gray morning. He saw Sprug grab a big handful of the woman's dress and lead her out into the light. She followed obediently, as if she weren't used to resisting. Or as if there were no strength left for resistance. *Probably both,* Tim thought. He hadn't known her name before he'd heard it on the stairs, but he'd seen Moira on the streets. He knew she was one of Jacques' girls. A prostitute and a junkie.

When Tim emerged from the stairway a few seconds later, he saw he wasn't actually on the roof, but on the top floor of the building. He stopped to brush a heavy coating of plaster dust off his blue jeans and then stamped his feet a couple times to knock what he could off his tan Western boots.

To his right, through two gaping holes in the wall where windows had once been, he could see a helter-skelter pattern of rooftops and chimneys. And far to the north stood the towering spire of one of Amsterdam's old churches—he couldn't tell which—rising out of the fog like a royal castle in a fairy-tale dream world.

The sound of a low moan behind him yanked Tim around. Moira had slumped against Sprug who was still gripping her arm. Beyond them was nothing but light and space;

the entire wall had been knocked out of the far end of the building.

Moira moaned again, but Sprug, his eyes now on Tim, made no reaction. A burly man in his forties, with gray hair and a beer-drinker's paunch, Sprug had maintained most of the strength he'd developed years before as a professional boxer. Even when he didn't move, his deliberate stance projected an air of physical confidence, a subtle belligerence befitting an experienced fighter.

Tim shivered. Partly in response to Sprug's look, but also because of a chilly breeze blowing through the exposed top floor of the old building. If Tim had known he was going to be outside, he'd at least have worn a sweatshirt instead of just a blue cotton t-shirt beneath his sleeveless denim jacket.

Tim was briskly rubbing his bare arms and hunching his shoulders against the cold when Jacques stepped out of the stairwell and into the light. The man, in his forties with black hair and a build that could be described as fashionably gaunt, smiled at Tim and donned the large reflective sunglasses he'd taken off to negotiate the building's dark interior. He wore a black silk dress shirt and a lavender tie, both of which seemed a little much for his cheap tan suit. And he deliberately licked a forefinger and bent down for just an instant to wipe off a single fleck of plaster clinging to one of his Gucci loafers.

"Hold this for me a minute please, Tim," Jacques said. And Tim reached out to take the cup and saucer. Nearly half a cup of warm, black coffee remained.

Tim stood riveted to the floor as Jacques crossed over toward Sprug and Moira. When Sprug released the woman, she stumbled and latched onto Jacques, who grasped her just above the elbows and held her out at arm's length. "You make problems, Moira," he said, his voice steady and softly calm. "You keep running away. Haven't we always taken good care of you?"

Moira nodded hesitantly.

Jacques held out his hand and Sprug pulled a syringe and needle from his jacket pocket—full and ready to shoot. "We're going to take care of you again," Jacques assured her.

Moira smiled weakly. And as she held out her arm, welcoming the needle, she turned her head and seemed to focus on Tim for the first time. Her dusky features and tall slender figure had probably once combined to give her an exotic sort of African allure. Traces of beauty remained beneath an aura of weariness. But the big eyes she fixed on Tim's seemed hollow, empty of all feeling. All life.

As Jacques jabbed the needle into her arm, her whole body jerked. Her eyes flashed with wild fear for an instant before they glazed over. The massive jolt of heroin had reached her brain. Jacques released her and handed the hypodermic back to Sprug. Moira raised her arms to the sky as if testing her hallucinatory wind. She staggered and then seemed to float across the floor toward the open end of the building.

Jacques talked to her in a soothing voice. "You want to fly, Moira? Is that it? You must because your wings are so beautiful and strong. Paris is straight ahead. You'll find love there."

As Moira lurched dangerously close to the floor's edge, Tim rushed toward her. But as he passed Jacques, the man snagged him by the jacket, stopping him. Coffee sloshed out of the cup and onto the saucer that Tim still held in his hand, but Tim's eyes never left Moira. A step away from the precipice she abrubtly whirled and began walking along the building's edge, her arms outstretched in imagined flight.

Jacques resumed his coaxing. "Oh, Calcutta. Is that what you see? You're free now, Moira. The door of your cage is open. Fly! Fly home. You can do it."

Suddenly she turned again and stepped out onto nothing. Tim instinctively shut his eyes, but not before he saw her drop out of sight, her arms flailing in the air. There was no scream. Just a sickening thud from far below.

When Tim forced his eyes open, he saw Jacques holding out his hand. When that action failed to register on Tim, Jacques pointed at the coffee. Tim numbly surrendered the cup and saucer, as Jacques gently chided him. "You spilled some, Tim. You must be more careful."

Tim turned to move toward the stairs, but Sprug clamped Tim's arm in a vicelike grip and moved him instead toward the edge where Moira had disappeared. A heart-pounding panic nearly overcame Tim. But as they neared the edge, Sprug loosed his grip and merely motioned him forward until Tim could see Moira sprawled on the ground below. Her neck and body and limbs twisted at grotesque angles.

Tim fought down a violent wave of nausea as Jacques stepped forward and took a final sip of coffee. "It's really too bad, Tim," he said, peering over the edge. "We were her family. But we got no respect from the lady. She wanted us to look after her, but she didn't want to fulfill her responsibilities."

Jacques shook his head slowly and then shrugged before turning to Tim and holding out his hand toward Sprug. Again Tim felt the panic surge, until he saw the plastic bag of hashish. Jacques passed Tim the bag, saying, "They are waiting for you out there, Tim. Your customers. I think you will do much business today."

Without risking a word, Tim stuffed the bag of hash into his pocket, turned and walked to the stairs where he hastily descended into the welcome darkness.

CHAPTER 2

The second he hit the street, Tim began to run. Back to the Amstel River and then north along the waterway toward the central city. He sprinted until his lungs burned and a calf muscle began to cramp and send screaming protests up his leg each time his right foot slammed against the pavement. The pain served to fill his mind, forcing out the fear and the images. *The flailing arms, the eyes.* So he ran on.

He knew he couldn't run forever. He had to think. But he needed to run. Back home he'd always done his best thinking after a three-mile workout up and down the beach, when he'd finally sprawl exhausted on the sand, listening to the soothing rhythm of the Pacific surf.

For a moment in his mind he could almost feel the warm California sand beneath his bare feet. But the hard, uneven reality of Amsterdam's cobblestone streets pounded home the truth. While luxuriously comfortable for daily wear, the calf-skin cowboy boots Aimee had given him as a graduation gift were definitely not designed for running. He could already feel a blister rising on his left heel.

Tim looked back over his shoulder. Seeing no sign of a yellow jeep, he slowed to a fast walk. Deciding not to take any chances, he crossed over to the east side of the river at the next bridge and then moved north again along the waterfront street marked "Weesperzijde."

The searing sensation in his lungs slowly subsided and the muscle knot in the leg worked itself out as he walked. But thinking about his boots had resurrected another pain, one that felt as strong now as it had six long weeks ago.

He sits in a chair in the biggest western store in the valley, trying on each pair of boots Aimee brings him. "These feel good," he finally says. Then he bends down and looks at the price tag. "Forget it!" he exclaims. There was no way he'd spend almost $200 for something to wear on his feet, no matter how good they looked or felt.

"I like them," she says. "They look great."

"They're too expensive."

"They'll be my gift," she says.

"No way," he protests. He knows the price represents almost three weeks' worth of work at the daycare center where she works part-time. But when he takes them off, she puts the boots back in their box and heads to the checkout counter with them while he's still pulling on his sneakers.

He argues as they wait for the sales clerk to wait on the woman in front of them. But Aimee insists. "It's a gift, Tim!" she says. And he finally gives up.

At her house a half hour later, she disappears into a back room for a few moments before returning with the boot box wrapped in the comic pages from a Sunday newspaper. "You have to accept this graciously," she instructs him. "And you have to act surprised."

He tears off the paper, opens the box, and lifts out the boots. "Just what I always wanted!"

As she rolls her eyes at his feigned surprise, he pulls her to him and kisses her. And they both laugh.

But they hadn't been laughing on the night before he'd left home.

They sit in the front seat of the car parked at the curb in front of her house. He brushes away her tears, wanting somehow to reassure her. "I have to go," he tells her as she buries her face against his shoulder.

She sits back up and looks into his face. "You keep saying you have to go. But why?"

He wants to explain because he wants her to understand. But it's so hard to put the feelings into words. The emotions have been buried so deep for so long that giving voice to them is hard. Painful and unsettling. But he wants Aimee to know, so he attempts to share what he feels, what he felt.

"I know a lot of people grow up without a father, but that doesn't make it any easier when you're ten years old and don't have a dad to play catch with you after supper. I always envied my friends whose fathers would take them camping or to ball games. Mom tried to do a lot of things with me, but it wasn't the same. I even envied the kids whose parents were divorced; I remember thinking, 'At least they have a father every other weekend!'"

Aimee reaches up and gently brushes at a tear he can feel trickling down his cheek. And he smiles at her a moment before he continues.

"Now I find out I might not have had to go through that. And that hurts even worse. If he's out there somewhere, I have to know. And to find out, I've got to go."

Aimee sniffles and he pulls her head onto his shoulder again. "I'll be fine," he reassures her. "And I'll be back before you know it.

"Actually," he continues, attempting a lighter tone, "you've got nothing to worry about. These boots you gave me are very special. I found an inspection card in the box that said, 'Fully guaranteed to bring any wandering cowboy safely

home to his true love.' I guess you could call it a 'honey back guarantee.'"

She groans at his pun, but she doesn't laugh. And the last thing she says to him that night, right after she kisses him a final goodbye, is, "Those boots better do their job."

The loud metallic clank of a tugboat butting against a river barge on the other side the Amstel pulled Tim's mind back to Amsterdam. And he suddenly felt farther from Aimee and home than he'd ever dreamed he could be. More than miles, more than a continent and an ocean separated them now. Much more.

He had to think. There had to be a way. The next street sign told him where he was: Oosterparkstraat. He turned away from the river toward the solitude he knew he'd find in Ooster Park this early in the day.

There wasn't any sandy beach. But for three hours Tim Devon lay on his back in the damp, watching the heavy gray morning sky gradually burn away to blue. The exertion had done its job. He was thinking, more clearly than he'd thought in weeks.

He'd been in Ooster Park once before. Right after he'd arrived in Amsterdam, back about the middle of May when the tulip gardens had been in full bloom. The colors had been spectacular. His dream had been so bright. Everything had been so exciting. For the first week he'd spent half of each day playing tourist, exploring the ancient streets, soaking in the sights and sounds and smells of Old Amsterdam. The other half day he'd devoted to beginning his search.

He'd never anticipated so many dead ends. Of course, he started with phone books and the phone company. Then he'd been to every post office branch in the city. When one of the clerks at the U.S. Consulate suggested a variant spelling, he'd gotten a new burst of hope that sent him doubling back over the same trail once again. By the start of his second week, he'd been spending all day, every day, on his quest. He'd pooled his graduation money and a major chunk of his savings, but despite the fact he was staying in the cheapest youth hostel he could find at ten guilders a night and eating only one real meal a day, his bankroll had shrunk fast. He'd cut his sleeping expenses in half by camping for four guilders a night when it didn't rain. But even so, by the end of week two, he'd estimated he could last only another week, maybe ten days. He gave up riding the buses and the trams and kept his pay phone calls to an absolute minimum. Still, all he'd found were dead ends. The dream was slowly fading.

It had begun to turn into a nightmare on the evening of June 1. He'd never forget the date. It'd been at the top of every one of the police forms he'd had to sign. He'd spent the afternoon in the reference section of the library looking fruitlessly for some sort of directory that could help. He was heading back to the campground when he took a shortcut to avoid the crowds congregating for an evening at the restaurants and nightclubs around Leidseplein. The backstreets were shadowed and empty. He didn't hear anything until someone grabbed him from behind and shoved him into the darkness of a narrow alley.

There were two men. It was too dark to see anything but silhouettes. One man held the point of a knife to Tim's side. The other one, speaking English with an accent that sounded middle-eastern, said, "We won't hurt you if you cooperate."

Tim had swallowed hard and croaked out a barely audible, "Okay." They'd taken his backpack with all his clothes, his camera, his wallet, his money. And thirty seconds later the men were sprinting away down the alley.

Somehow they had missed his watch. And fortunately he'd left his return plane ticket in his guitar case, stowed away in one of the lockers at Central Station for the night. And his assailants didn't get his passport which he carried tucked down in the top of his boot. Safely inside the passport was a folded page from an old yearbook. The muggers had at least left him that hope. Not that it mattered after they'd taken all the money needed to continue the search.

He'd had to wait for almost two hours at the Elandsgracht police headquarters; there was a line of people ahead of him. The officer who finally took down his statement and a description of his losses had been professional, if not particularly sympathetic. When Tim recounted what had happened, the man reminded him about the crime warning signs posted in five languages at the train station and suggested that in the future he stick to the main thoroughfares at night. The officer explained to Tim where to find the nearest American Express office and when Tim admitted he'd been carrying cash, not traveler's checks, the officer shook his head and muttered something in Dutch that sounded a bit to Tim like, "Don't leave home without it!" He suggested Tim check back in a day or two to see if anything turned up, but Tim knew there would be no use.

Even as Tim descended the steps of the police station, he'd begun to wonder where he could get a KLM schedule to find the next open flight back to the States. That's when he heard the voice behind him calling, "Hey, you! Amerikaan. Wacht even! Wait a minute."

There should have been a warning sign saying, "Beware of strangers at police stations." But there wasn't. And Tim hadn't learned until much later that this man who introduced himself as Jacques had been at the station for questioning himself, something to do with the beating of a suspected drug dealer.

"I overheard some of your story as you told it to the officer," Jacques said. "Perhaps I can help. I know a very cheap but clean hotel. Just twenty guilders for the night and breakfast tomorrow." He held out two 10 guilder notes.

Tim shook his head. "I don't have any way to pay you back. And I'll probably have to fly home tomorrow if I can. All I have left is my airline ticket."

This unexpected benefactor tucked the bills in Tim's shirt pocket, smiled, and shrugged. "I'll just have to trust you for it." He gave Tim an address and said, "Come and see me here in the morning and perhaps you can pay me back by delivering a few messages for me."

The next morning he'd found Jacques at a little cafe on the Zeedijk, at the edge of the oldest part of the city. After commending Tim for his integrity, Jacques insisted on loaning Tim enough to replace his lost pack and clothes. Tim agreed to let Jacques hold his plane ticket as collateral against the loan and immediately took on the job of part-time messenger. Every morning he showed up at the cafe to meet Jacques. Sometimes there would be five or six messages to deliver around the city. Other days, only a couple envelopes to give to a shopkeeper or a waiter in some cafe. Sometimes he'd just meet one of Jacques' associates on a predetermined street corner. Occasionally there'd be a message to carry back to the cafe. But always he was done by noon and had the afternoons free to continue his search.

At the start Tim had naïvely assumed Jacques was merely a businessman. But after a few days of seeing the kinds of people who frequented Jacques' table at the Zeedijk cafe, Tim knew Jacques' businesses included prostitution and drugs. But he also knew without Jacques he'd have to give up his search and go home. And this was after all, Amsterdam. While it wasn't the wide-open city it had been in the '60s and '70s numerous cafes still posted the price of various grades of marijuana on the wall next to the menu. Then there was the Walletjes, the oldest part of the inner city, the red-light district, where prostitution was sanctioned as it had been in Amsterdam since the 14th century.

So who was he to judge Jacques. Especially when Jacques had been so generous with him—not only staking him with an advance to replace his clothes and gear, but later loaning the cash to cover the train fare for that cross-country, wild-goose chase to Nijmegen when Tim thought he'd turned up a real lead. Sure, Jacques had asked to hold Tim's passport the three days he was gone. But he'd always trusted Tim and never directly involved him in anything Tim thought was illegal.

Until this morning when Tim had witnessed Moira's death. *Moira's murder.* No one had pushed her. So when her body was found it would probably be termed a suicide or a simple overdose. The Amsterdam police saw a lot of those every year.

But it had been murder, just as certain as it had been a warning to him. He'd been playing on the fringes of a dangerous game for almost a month. Now suddenly he'd been shoved into the action. And he was caught.

The crazy dream that had brought him to Amsterdam was over. Now all he wanted was to get out. And there was only one way. Jacques had made that very clear both in what he'd done and in what he'd said. *I think you will do much business today.*

Tim jumped to his feet and walked briskly out of Ooster Park, heading northwest toward the city's center. It was the only way home.

They're waiting for you out there, Tim.

His customers.

He just had to find them.

CHAPTER 3

The Boeing 747 had lifted off in darkness from New Delhi early the night before. It had landed to refuel once somewhere in the Mideast before dawn. So it wasn't until the clouds below began to break and scatter as the plane started its descent into Amsterdam that Rajam Prasad got his first real sensation of flying.

Mysterious ribbons of flashing silver seemed to lace the land together 25,000 feet below. At 15,000 feet Rajam realized he was seeing the midday sun reflecting off the water of an incredibly complex network of canals and rivers that crossed and crisscrossed the land, dividing The Netherlands into irregular geometric patterns of brown and green.

Flying was even more amazing than Rajam's friends had told him it would be. At 10,000 feet he could see roads, buildings, a train moving ever so slowly. It looked like a map or a miniature model stretching out below. He was seeing the world for the first time through the eyes of an eagle. *Or, perhaps,* he thought, *through the eyes of God.*

The sense of awe he experienced as he pressed his face against the cool glass of the aircraft's window reminded him of a feeling he hadn't had since he was an eight-year-old boy. When he took his first and only childhood train ride, a family pilgrimage from Lucknow to the holy city of Varanasi for the Festival of Lights. His parents had spent all their meager savings to purchase passage for themselves and their six children. The second-class tickets entitled his family to crowd into the metal racks that hung from the ceiling of the passenger car, just above the heads of the travelers already occupying the seats below. Everything about that trip, from the noisy, belching steam engine, to the ritual bath in the sacred Ganges River at Varanasi, had seemed an unbelievable adventure to a small boy from an impoverished village in the state of Uttar Pradesh.

Compared to that highlight of his childhood which he now remembered with a touch of sadness, an airplane flight, especially an airplane flight to the great city of Amsterdam in the country of The Netherlands, seemed like a miracle. But then Rajam Prasad believed in miracles.

# # #

Tim hurried through the usual noonday crush of humanity in downtown Amsterdam during tourist season. Impatiently he wound his way through the jammed sidewalks along the Damrak toward his destination of Central Station. From time to time he'd try to circumvent an immobile throng by moving into the street itself and picking his way through the traffic and down the middle of the street in the no-man's land between the trams.

Despite the constant cacophony of automobile horns, the click and clatter of electric trams, and the hordes of jet-setting tourists, much of 20th-century Amsterdam remains an ancient city. Narrow 17th-century streets winding along canals and over more than 1,000 bridges, many of which are drawbridges, reduce the movement in this most "progressive" of cities to the tempo of barges and bicycles.

For Tim Devon it was a frustrating pace. He needed to make the most of the rest of the day. He needed to find his customers.

Finally he reached the intersection of Damrak and Prins Hendrikkade, just a bridge and the plaza between him and the massive architectural façade of Central Station. There, on the plaza, among the milling crowds, he would begin looking for his customers. They were always there. The railroad station and a thousand trains a day guaranteed it.

Crossing between the rows of buses and trams that perpetually lined the thoroughfares in front of the train station, Tim surveyed the crowd. One cluster of people surrounded a mime troup acting out a comic scene. At the far end of the plaza, a Salvation Army band finished a jazzy rendition of "When the Saints Go Marching In," and most of their audience began to disperse as a uniformed officer stepped up onto a box and began to talk to the crowd. Always there were masses of people at the station and almost always there were those wishing to entertain or exhort those masses.

Then Tim saw what he was looking for. Two girls. Americans with money. Their new clothes and the backpacks fresh out of an L. L. Bean catalog told him Amsterdam was probably their first stop on a European adventure. *A couple preppies. Right out of some New England college for women,* he guessed, stopping a couple of paces behind them.

The shorter girl, whose long blonde hair made him think for a moment of Aimee, pulled a small handful of change out of her pocket and dropped it into a tin can. At the sound, a black man, dressed in a white evening jacket and standing on a pyramid of three wooden crates turned with the exaggerated jerkiness of a robot to face the girls. "Thank-you-ladies," he said in a robotlike baritone with a Jamaican accent. He then froze in another position and Tim noticed the cardboard sign propped against the boxes: "Human Statue."

The girls were laughing. Tim made his move.

"Hi," he said, walking up beside them. "Where's home?"

"Why? Is this a poll?" the blonde asked.

"I'm from the West Coast. A California boy just hoping for a friendly face." He hoped his attempted nonchalance masked the nervousness he felt. He didn't want to spook his first customers.

"How can you be lonely? This is Amsterdam."

"He must be some kind of official greeter," the brunette finally spoke. "Are you paid to do this?"

"Yeah, sure," Tim replied with sarcasm, trying to read the girls and deciding to make a pitch. "Actually, my dad's an actor. If I dropped his name, you'd squeal. He pulled my allowance and kicked me over to Europe to learn about life."

He paused and looked around before he continued. "But I've got some great hash—really primo. Guaranteed to make Amsterdam 'memorable.'"

Tim noticed a look of uncertainty pass between the two girls. "You're in luck to buy from me. If you don't know your sources, the stuff in this town can be very dirty."

The cynical preppie looked him in the eye as she instructed her friend, "Talk price with the scumbag, Sally. I'll just be a minute."

"Don't mind her," the blonde said apologetically as the other girl walked off. "She's all mouth. You get used to it."

"I wouldn't!" Tim said, turning to watch the girl walking across the plaza. Suddenly she stopped and said something to a mounted police officer, as if she were asking instructions. Then she turned and pointed toward Tim.

Tim bolted, hurdling a stack of suitcases and heading for the thickest part of the throng by the tram stops at the end of the plaza. He heard the blonde's voice calling, "Don't go! It's only a test!" But he didn't slow down, he didn't even look back as he dodged through the crowd.

#

Despite the smooth landing, as he stepped out of the jet-way and into the arrival gate at Schiphol International Airport, Rajam Prasad barely resisted the urge to fall on his face and kiss the ground. He was in Amsterdam. That in itself seemed like a miracle.

For a minute he just stood and listened to the sound of languages surrounding him. From some of those welcoming his fellow passengers at the gate he heard the familiar strains of Hindi and Urdu and a couple other Indian dialects—he guessed Punjabi and Bengali. There was a public address announcement in Dutch. A smattering of English, of course. And one old woman greeting another in what he guessed was French or Spanish. For someone who'd never before left Indian soil, it seemed more than his senses could soak in.

The amplified words of a man carrying a small megaphone didn't even register until the third or fourth time he heard them. "Amsterdam 86 participants. Amsterdam 86. All those attending the International Conference for Itinerant Evangelists come this way, please." Rajam approached the man making the announcement and was quickly joined by a dozen others from the New Delhi flight. He'd had no idea there were other conference delegates aboard, but he wasn't really surprised. The letters he had received about the conference said there would be more than 7,500 participants from around the world. Many Indians would be there, of course.

Rajam quickly introduced himself all around. And as the ICIE steward who'd greeted them led the group toward the baggage claim area, Rajam noted that he, at age twenty-five, seemed by far the youngest in the contingent of his countrymen. Another humbling reminder of what it meant for him to be in Amsterdam.

As he followed the guide and his new acquaintances onto a moving walkway and felt the odd sensation of riding a moving floor, Rajam grinned in amazement and joy. He was still grinning when he noticed the mirror along the far wall. His own image seemed to float down the corridor, an almost perfect reflection of his inner feelings. He was in Amsterdam. And it was indeed a miracle.

# # #

Just before he ducked around the corner of a building, Tim ventured a quick look back. He saw no policeman. Maybe it had been a test or just an attempt by the mouthy girl to get rid of him. But then again, if the policeman had dismounted to follow him through the crowd, Tim might not have spotted him. And he couldn't take that chance.

Suddenly slowing to a fast walk that he hoped would draw less attention, Tim scanned the street. Ten paces ahead he saw what he needed. When he reached the trash receptacle bolted to a large post, he stopped and casually leaned against it. The trash can's plastic liner was almost empty—it wouldn't be emptied again until the next morning.

Again checking up and down the street for observers, Tim knelt and extracted the plastic packet from the top of his boot. As he stood, he pushed the package of hashish through the springdoor in the top of the trash container and let it drop. Looking around once more but noting no staring or curious eyes, Tim once again started down the street away from Central Station. He could still feel his heart pumping and his pulse racing; his adrenalin supply was getting a test today. But he hadn't panicked. Fewer than sixty seconds had passed since that girl had pointed him out to the policeman. He was safe. And his stash was safe until he came back for it in the evening.

Everything was going to be fine. There would be more customers at night.

# # #

Rajam Prasad stood in the lobby of the Schiller Hotel, certain there'd been some misunderstanding. The conference material he had received in India had said many participants would be sleeping in large rooms, dormitory style, with rows and rows of beds. But the polished, dark-stained paneling surrounding him and the chandelier hanging above his head were not dormitory trappings.

"No mistake, Mr. Prasad," said the desk clerk, looking up from his computer terminal. "You are in Room 412. There's one other gentleman registered for that room. But he's not scheduled to arrive until later this evening. Here's your room key. Just follow the bellboy. He'll get your bags and show you to your room. Please, enjoy your stay with us."

Rajam turned around to see a short man in a uniform, a gentleman who looked to be fifty or sixty years old, walking across the lobby with the battered brown cardboard suitcase Rajam's American Bible professor had loaned him for the trip. The young Indian tried to grab his suitcase back, but the man said something in Dutch and held on.

A door slid open in front of them and Rajam followed the man inside. The man pushed a button, the doors closed, and Rajam gasped at the unexpected sensation of his first elevator ride. When the bellboy glanced at him, Rajam smiled in embarrassment and watched the lighted numbers on the transom trace their upward progress.

The elevator stopped, and the bellboy walked out into the fourth floor hallway with the suitcase. Feeling awkward to be served in such a manner by a man as old as his own father, Rajam tried again to reclaim his bag: "Is it not too heavy for you?"

Once more the bellboy wrestled the suitcase away from the Indian, swearing under his breath in Dutch because he knew he wouldn't get a tip from this foreigner.

# # #

After walking around the city streets for an hour, Tim surveyed the plaza from in front of a cafe across the street from Central Station. The girls were gone. No sign of the policeman. So Tim crossed the bridge, picked his way through the crowd and entered the cavernous old station. There he found the familiar bank of luggage lockers from which he retrieved his backpack. And he also pulled out a well-worn guitar case and strapped it to his pack frame with a red and green bungee cord.

For the remainder of the afternoon he would look like a sightseeing college kid, backpacking his way around the continent. But since he didn't feel like acting the part, he found a bit of solitude on some empty steps leading down to a small canal on a quiet backstreet. He took his old Martin guitar from its case and began to strum, leaving the case propped open. And as he played he studied the pictures of Aimee he'd taped inside the top. But none of the sad bluesy tunes that came to his mind even began to reflect the loneliness he felt as the sun cast longer and longer shadows across the canal.

When his watch said six o'clock, Tim packed up again and headed for his stash. He stood at the corner nearest the trash container for ten minutes, watching the street, studying the passersby. Satisfied there was no surveillance, he walked over and casually threw away a tourist brochure about canal boat tours. Then as if changing his mind, he reached into the container, through the day's debris to the very bottom.

It isn't there! But it has to be! He groped around. *Nothing.* He yanked out the liner so he could see the terrible truth. The entire stash of drugs Jacques had given him was gone.

CHAPTER 4

As dusk settled over Amsterdam, Rembrandtsplein's myriad of neon lights already bathed the square in fantasy hues of pink and yellow and blue. The usual evening multitude had begun to gather at the center of Amsterdam's world-renowned nightlife. The flashing signs not only cast their light, but they gave the scene, and the streets themselves, a beating, pulsing life.

Traveling businessmen, curious tourists and native Amsterdamers crowded the sidewalks beneath the advertisements for a plethora of cabarets, floor shows, nightclubs, and topless bars. And scattered around the central square, standing near the curb where they could see into and be seen from the slowly cruising cars, were a couple dozen young boys. And a few not so young. From time to time one of them would bend over at an open car window, and exchange a few words with the driver before climbing in and riding away.

Tim wanted to avoid the lights of Rembrandtsplein, but the shortest course to his destination cut through one corner of the square. So he ducked his head and stayed out of the brightest glare. He was half a block past the square when he heard a voice behind him calling, "Hey, Tim. Ease up, man."

It was Wouter, a German guy just a few years older than Tim. He worked some of the time for Jacques, selling drugs. But he'd been friendly with Tim. And he'd been the one person in Amsterdam that Tim had confided in and told the real reason for his coming in the first place.

Wouter motioned for Tim to wait a minute. Then he slipped what looked like a small packet of coke out of his pocket and handed it to a teen-age boy in exchange for a handful of bills.

"Hi, Wouter," Tim said as the young dealer walked toward him. "How's it going?"

"You got a plane to catch, Tim? Or you got time for a beer?"

Tim liked Wouter. Maybe he could help. But Tim wasn't ready to talk. And he wanted no connection with Jacques tonight.

"Business," Tim lied, backing away as if he had to hurry. "I've got a sale going down."

Wouter shrugged. "Just stay away from the Dam tonight. Too many narcs in leather jackets."

"Thanks. Catch you later." Tim turned to go and then stopped to call back, "Don't tell Jacques you ran into me, okay?"

"Trouble?"

"No . . . but I'll owe you one."

Tim headed off down the street. He didn't look back to see the curious, unconvinced look on Wouter's face as he stood and watched Tim hurry away.

#

In Room 412 of the Schiller Hotel, a four-star inn facing onto Rembrantsplein, Rajam Prasad was lying quietly on his bed. His eyes scanned the decor for the hundredth time, taking in the rich brown paneling, the draperies, the brass lamp, the paintings hanging on the wall. He still couldn't believe the luxury of his incredible good fortune.

He sat up and looked at the still figure of Abraham Abimue, his African roommate, who had curiously spread a blanket over the carpeting and was now lying on the floor beside his bed. The friendly Kenyan, who Rajam guessed was somewhere between forty and fifty years of age, had arrived only an hour before. They had introduced themselves and shared a little small talk, enough for Rajam to realize his new friend struggled with English, before they both agreed they were tired and ought to get a good night's sleep prior to the start of the conference the next morning.

For a moment Rajam thought his roommate had already drifted off to sleep. But the African opened his eyes and smiled to see Rajam's curious face. "I wait for heaven . . . maybe sleep on soft bed there," he said. "Lord must give new back first."

Rajam grinned in response. "You are in the West now, Brother Abraham. It is the custom."

Abraham shrugged and shook his head. Then he sat up. "You have camera? Click! Click!" He pantomimed a photographer snapping a picture.

"I did. But it broke."

"Too bad," the African responded. "I like show picture to my village." He motioned around the room. "Only rich man live in palace . . . my country."

Rajam nodded his understanding. "This is the West."

# # #

Tim shoved his backpack, then his guitar case, up onto the corrugated metal roof of the old shed before pulling himself up after them. From the top of the shed he crawled onto a concrete ledge back under the train trestle now just a couple feet above his head. He'd discovered this refuge just a week or so earlier, on a rainy night when the campgrounds were full. And he'd returned every night since, using the extra guilders he saved for food.

At the mere thought of food, an empty, aching stomach reminded him that he hadn't eaten all day. With everything else that happened, it hadn't seemed important. He'd gotten used to a little hunger during the past few weeks as he'd conditioned himself to the one good meal a day he could afford. But now, at the end of the most physically and emotionally trying day in his life, he felt famished.

Too tired to risk the dark streets again in search of a supper he could afford, Tim promised himself two meals tomorrow as he unrolled and crawled into his sleeping bag. Despite a racing mind replaying the horror of his day, Tim soon fell into a fitful sleep.

He sits slumped in the depths of a deep-cushioned easy chair. The new designer couch, with its bright floral pattern, is nothing but a shadowy silhouette in the darkened living room. He stares at nothing until car lights sweep across the room and he focuses on the door.

A key scrapes into the lock. The deadbolt slides free and the door opens. A lamp flicks on.

"Tim!" the woman gasps, almost dropping the bag she had clamped under her arm as she extracted the key from the lock. "You startled me so. Why are you sitting in the dark?"

She looks so professional, so perfect in her yellow pantsuit with the complementary white jacket. She's as pretty as she always is, looking so much younger than her thirty-eight years that she's often mistaken for his sister, instead of his mother. But Tim remains silent, watching her walk into the room.

"Don't be in a mood, Tim. I'm sorry I'm late. But I've got a great reason . . ." She pauses, smiling, baiting him to respond. When he doesn't, she goes on. "I closed that Riverdale property today and the office insisted on hauling out the

champagne to celebrate."

She puts the bag she has been carrying on the coffee table and bends down to kiss him on the top of his head and then playfully tousles his hair. Straightening up, she grins proudly. "My commission will more than cover your first year of college. How about that? Not bad for an old lady, huh?"

Still no response.

"Tim, what is it?"

"What's what?"

"What's with the silent treatment? And what's that funny look on your face?"

"I guess I was just trying to decide about you."

"If this is a game, I don't get it," she says, collecting the sack and her purse and heading for the kitchen. "But I did get Chinese for supper. Peapod beef, your favorite."

He follows her, stopping in the kitchen doorway as she puts the take-out cartons on the table and quickly sets two places. She tosses him a cellophane-wrapped fortune cookie as she asks, "Well, how was your day?"

"Nothing special," he finally says, watching her place one pair of red plastic chopsticks next to each plate. "I just found out that I'm a bastard and my mother may be the world's biggest liar."

The words, and even more, his quiet, bitter tone hit her hard. All the excitement of her day is knocked out of her. He hears it in her sigh and the deep breath she takes before she says, "Maybe you should start at the beginning."

The stricken look on her face tells him everything else he needs to know. It was all true.

Without another word he wheels and walks out of the kitchen.

Somewhere in the distance a church bell marked the hour and Tim rolled over in his sleeping bag.

# # #

Rajam felt too excited to sleep. Seeing his roommate also awake, he ventured a question to Abraham. "I wonder why the hotel provided us with a telephone. Do you have friends to ring up?"

The African's response reflected his surprise and puzzlement. "Oh, no, brother. I sorry."

Rajam picked up the receiver and checked for the dial tone. A few seconds later a voice surprised him. "Who am I calling, please?" he asked.

A moment later he whispered an explanation to Abraham. "The hotel operator wishes us a very good evening."

Abraham smiled and nodded as Rajam again spoke into the phone. "My friend Abraham and I do not know anyone in Amsterdam to call. So if you need the telephone in our room, please be so kind to take it." He listened for a moment and then added, "And a pleasant night's sleep to you as well."

Hanging up the receiver, he turned to Abraham and explained the exchange. "She assures us the hotel will not need our telephone while we are here. She says the hotel has many."

"The West . . ." Abraham shook his head as Rajam turned off the bedside light.

In the darkness Abraham speaks again. "My children know not where can be Holland. On wall I fix map. Each night before sleeping they touch map and send love and prayers to me, yeh?" He paused as if in thought for a few moments. "Your family, Rajam? They pray good for you here?"

The young Indian couldn't bring himself to respond. So he stirred slightly and pretended to be asleep already.

# # #

Under the railroad trestle, Tim tossed and turned in the darkness, trying in vain to find a comfortable position on his concrete slab.

He's taking the stairs three at a time but he can hear her right behind him. She's just a few steps behind as he enters his room. There's pain and anger in her voice.

"We've had it good. And I'm proud of that. You can't make it something dirty, Tim. I won't let you."

He picks up a framed photograph from the dresser. He doesn't turn around, but he can see in the mirror that his mother has stopped just inside the doorway. "I talked to this picture when I was a kid," he says. "I told 'Dad' all the stuff I couldn't say to you. Where did you come up with this guy? Did you just cut him out of some magazine?"

He watches in the mirror as she winces and implores him, "Tim, please . . ."

"Please what, Mother?" Then sarcastically he adds, "I assume you are my mother."

She sits on the end of his bed, crying now. "He was just a friend. Someone I truly loved and admired. But it was a long time ago now. And we're not . . ."

"Not what?"

"Not the same people."

At that, he whirls around to face her. "Oh, yeah? Easy for you to say. Maybe that works for you. But I don't know WHO I am anymore." He hurls the picture against the bedroom wall. The glass shatters.

The violent clatter and the shaking that jerked Tim upright in the darkness were deafening and disorienting. Until he recognized the clack-clacking rumble of a freight train crossing the steel trestle just inches above his head. That's when the thought struck him. He'd been awakened from one nightmare only to find himself in another. And both of them were real.

CHAPTER 5

The morning sunlight that flooded the room after Abraham opened the drapes found Rajam Prasad carefully remaking his bed. He fluffed his pillow and meticulously straightened the spread, being certain to brush out even the slightest wrinkle. And while Abraham sat on the edge of his own bed to buckle his sandals, Rajam picked up the telephone and waited almost a full minute before responding, "And a very good morning to you also. This is Mr. Prasad in Room 412. My friend Mr. Abimue and I will be leaving soon to attend the International Conference for Itinerant Evangelists taking place at the Rai Center. We wanted you to know we will be gone all day."

He paused. "Is that true? Brother Abraham and I thank you for your most kind invitation!" Replacing the phone, he turned to his African brother. "The hotel operator invites us to a special breakfast downstairs before we go."

Abraham grins and shakes his head in amazement. "Hallelujah."

A half hour later, after a breakfast of rolls, thin slices of cheese and ham, a boiled egg and two cups of the richest coffee they had ever tasted, Rajam and Abraham headed across the lobby for the hotel entrance. The elevator doors slid open and a cluster of Africans walked out in front of them. Abraham recognized a fellow countryman and there were excited introductions all around.

After meeting everyone in the group, Rajam separated himself from the friendly din, saying to Abraham, "I will walk ahead, brother. I have charted my course." As his roommate nods and waves, the Indian strode out the door and into the street.

Five minutes and a dozen blocks later, Rajam stops at a busy intersection and checks his map. He noted the signs, pronounced the long Dutch street names and quickly found his location on his map. He'd learned to read all kinds of maps during his two-year stint in the Indian army and that training was serving him well now. He marched confidently on until the street turned abruptly at a canal and the next street posting wasn't on the map.

Frustrated and a little confused, he was considering retracing his steps to the hotel to ask new directions when he spotted a young man with a backpack and a guitar who walked as if he knew where he was going. Rajam hurried across the street to ask for help.

# # #

Tim Devon had to stop when an Indian, dressed in white linen trousers and a white knee-length shirt, stepped into his path and poised his hands together in what looked like some kind of formal salute.

"Namaskaram. A greeting from my country which means 'Good wishes to you.'"

Tim stepped around him and continued walking. He didn't have time for any distraction this morning. But the Indian began trotting after him and talking.

"Pardon, please. I am seeking the Rai Center. I was told it was exactly a fifteen-minute walk from my hotel. But if I retrace my steps I could be tardy for the opening session of the great International Conference for Itinerant Evangelists. And this would clearly be an insult to my hosts."

Rajam scurried up beside Tim and offered his hand. "I am Rajam Prasad. My Western friends call me Raj. My country is India. And to be in your beautiful city is proof that with God all things are possible."

Tim looked again at the smiling Indian. He saw breakfast and he stopped. "Could you spare a few guilders, sir? I'm really hungry. Last night some guys jumped me in the park and cleaned me out. Wallet, traveler's checks, everything!"

"Oh, you are American, yes?"

Tim nodded. "My gut is in knots, man. I'm so hungry." He finally extended his hand. "Tim Devon."

Raj smiled. "Thanks God, they didn't take your pack or your beautiful guitar, Timothy."

"I'd hidden them in some bushes or they would have. I tried to hold them off, but there were six of them . . ."

"I am sorry," Raj said. "I once played the guitar myself at school. It was my most favored instrument. I learned a popular song from the United States. Perhaps you know it? 'Homeland on the Range'?"

Ignoring the question, Tim pressed his case. "Just ten guilders. I have to get something to eat. I'll pay you back. I'll bring it to your hotel after the American Express office opens this morning."

Raj frowned. "It shames me not to meet your request. I never dreamed to find anyone hungry in Amsterdam. I have no guilders. But I will go in search of food for you."

Judging the encounter a complete waste of time, Tim turned and walked away. "Forget it," he said over his shoulder.

# # #

As he watched the young American retreat down the street, Raj called after him. "I will return to this street corner at the first possible moment, Timothy. I will bring food. You can trust my best intentions for you."

Tim never looked back. The American boy's story couldn't help but remind Raj of the biblical parable of the good Samaritan. So, as he resumed his own trek, he carried with him a strong sense of failure that he hadn't been able to help a needy stranger. He also felt a twinge of guilt as he recalled his own "free" breakfast.

# # #

The prospect of conning a breakfast from that naïve, talkative Indian had awakened Tim's empty stomach. He had to have something to eat. Anything.

A few minutes later a paneled bakery truck passed him and stopped at the curb in the next block. The driver got out, leaving his engine idling, and opened the back where he slid out an entire rack of fresh bread—long French-style loaves and sweet rolls. When the delivery man hoisted the rack to his shoulder and headed toward the door of a small cafe, Tim picked up his pace. The man would be out quickly for another load, or he wouldn't have left the rear door of his truck wide open. But Tim figured he had a few seconds because the bakery man would have to take the bread to the kitchen.

As Tim stepped off the curb to the back of the open bakery truck, the yeasty aroma of fresh-baked bread started his mouth watering. He looked toward the open door of the cafe. *No one in sight.* Leaning quickly into the truck he made a split-second breakfast decision. He grabbed one long warm loaf and was reaching for a broodje to stick in his pocket when he heard an angry shout from the cafe. He looked up to see the cafe owner standing inside the window waving his arms.

Tim was halfway down the block on a dead run by the

time a screaming baker charged out of the cafe and jumped into his truck. When Tim heard the gearbox grind and the motor race, he glanced back over his shoulder to see the truck barrelling down on him.

Tim sprinted for his life, looking for a break between the houses lining the narrow street. *There. An alley on the right.* Tim ducked into it as the truck's brakes squealed. The man was backing up and turning into the alley.

When he hit the next street, Tim took a quick left, dodging cars at the next intersection and racing for the safety of the park just beyond it. But the bakery truck, its horn blaring, slammed through the intersection and skidded to a halt at the edge of the park. And Tim looked back to see the driver bounding out of the truck and coming after him on foot.

The man, despite being older and a bit on the pudgy side, was gaining. Tim was nearly winded. The baker was fresh and very angry. Trying not to break stride, Tim slipped off his pack and his guitar and flung them into some bushes just off the path. He had to concentrate on speed. His pursuer was slowing, but continuing the chase. Tim couldn't believe the guy was expending so much energy over a lousy loaf of bread.

The bread. He still clutched the loaf in his hand like a fat relay baton. He tore a huge chunk off the loaf with his teeth and tossed the rest aside as he ran.

Ahead was a street. And a canal bridge. Tim looked back to see his pursuer had stopped and doubled over to catch his breath. Tim slowed to a walk. But the sight of his slowing quarry gave the man a second wind and the chase resumed.

As he neared the bridge, Tim saw his chance. If he could get there in time. He did. In the middle of the bridge he stopped and clambered over the railing. Then looking back at the red-faced baker charging after him, Tim let go and jumped.

He landed with a resounding thud on the deck of the moving barge six feet below. The captain of the tug towing the barge looked back and began screaming and gesturing for him to get off. Tim nodded and yelled back that he'd get off at the next bridge. Then he turned back and saluted the baker who was standing helplessly on the bridge behind, waving a fist and swearing in Dutch.

CHAPTER 6

To Raj, it looked as if the entire world had reached the Rai Center ahead of him. And indeed, delegates from around the globe milled and mingled throughout the massive outer corridors. For a few minutes he just stood and watched with fascination, trying to guess many nationalities, or at least home continents, by the color of the faces or by the national dress. He checked his guesses by reading the name tags of those who passed nearby: Korea; Surinam; Italy; Honduras; Thailand; Norway; Lebanon; Ethiopia; Bolivia; Papua New Guinea; Republic of Palau, and many more.

Realizing that he didn't yet have his own official conference identification, Rajam set out in search of the registration tables. The long, slow-moving lines proved easy to find. And the boisterous atmosphere, electric with anticipation, made Raj's prolonged wait seem much shorter than it was. On every side people joyously greeted old friends and introduced themselves to new ones. Raj found himself offering "Namaskarams" right and left.

#

After waiting until he figured it was safe, Tim doubled back toward the park where he'd ditched his gear. Recrossing the bridge he'd jumped from, he noticed a figure walking along the canal carrying what looked like . . . Tim stopped and looked to be sure before he yelled, "Hey, you!"

When the guy failed to respond, Tim sprinted to the other side of the bridge, slid down the embankment, and ran along the canal after the retreating figure. "Hey, man! That's mine!"

As Tim closed in, the guy turned to face him. Tim suddenly realized his quarry stood a head taller than he did and was built like a linebacker. Streaks of orange and pink paint highlighted his spiked hair. The punker's eyes betrayed a streak of meanness on the inside.

"The guitar," Tim said, anyway. "It's mine."

"I found it," the punk said. "Nobody around. And I gotta raise some cash." He turned to walk away.

"I can prove it's mine. The pictures. They're all over the inside of the lid. My girlfriend. Just open it. You'll see."

As the guy turned again to face Tim, he reached inside his coat and pulled out the pictures of Aimee. He smiled and flicked them into the canal. "No pictures."

Tim leaped at the thief—like a terrier taking on a bear. But the big guy was ready. He swung a meaty forearm into Tim's face, sending him crashing to the ground. Then he turned and walked casually away.

Tasting blood in his mouth, Tim jumped to his feet and charged after his foe, whaling with his fists. The guy dropped the guitar and retreated a few steps in the force of Tim's fury. Then he grabbed Tim, swung him around and locked him in a stranglehold.

His windpipe cut off, his head wrenched back, Tim realized his opponent might actually break his neck. In desperation he kicked back with all his might. His hard, heavy cowboy boot hammered into a kneecap. The big guy screamed and loosed his grip just enough for Tim to twist free.

The two combatants stood facing each other, breathing hard. Knowing he needed an advantage, Tim made his move.

The momentum of his charge carried them both tumbling back, off the wall of the canal. For a long moment they were airborne. The impact knocked the wind out of Tim as the cold polluted water closed over them and filled Tim's eyes and ears and mouth. Down, down, down. An eternity passed before he reversed direction and kicked upward. He thought his lungs would explode before he regained the surface gasping and coughing up foul-tasting water.

No sooner had he gotten one sweet gulp of air than he felt two big hands clamp around his neck and force him back under. Somehow he reached up, found a handful of hair, and yanked down at the same time he jerked his own head back, his skull smashing against a nose and jaw.

Suddenly he was free and kicking for the surface again. When he broke into the light, Tim spotted his foe pulling himself up an old rope hanging from the canal wall. Knowing he couldn't get out of the canal before the thief reached his guitar and fled, Tim could only tread water and watch as the punker dragged himself up onto the bank. Then, incredibly, the guy simply staggered away, walking right past the guitar case as if it weren't there.

Tim retrieved three photos of Aimee floating in the canal before swimming to the rope and hauling himself up and over the canal wall. He still had to face Jacques and tell him about the lost hash. But as he sat on the canal bank, dumping the water out of his boots, Tim finally knew what he was going to say.

# # #

Raj lingered in the crowded corridor outside the Rai Center's enormous Europahal as the mid-morning break period came to an end. As the lines diminished, he made his third pass by the coffee table to pick up another couple of bananas and an orange. His pockets already bulged with fruit and rolls.

Then returning through the doors to the great hall, he spotted Abraham Abimue. Raj called out a greeting and when the African joined him, Raj explained what he was doing. Nodding solemnly, Abraham handed Raj another orange.

# # #

Tim strolled into the Zeedijk cafe, Jacques' daytime office, to find the dealer seated at his usual table, concentrating on his breakfast. One of his girls sat across the table from him, gesturing wildly and exclaiming loudly in Dutch. Jacques wasn't even looking at her.

Sprug, playing a game of solitaire at a nearby table, kicked out a chair and motioned Tim to sit and wait. Finally Jacques took a long sip of coffee and said something sharply to the girl. She knocked over her chair as she jumped to her feet. And she was still complaining as she stormed out of the cafe. Tim watched her go, wishing he knew what her angry recital was all about.

Sprug snapped his fingers and motioned Tim toward Jacques who was busy pouring a small lake of apple syrup over the last half of a spekpannekoek, a thick, fluffy Dutch pancake chock full of crisp bits of bacon. Tim tried to force his attention away from the plate as Jacques said, without looking up, "I expected you earlier this morning, Tim."

"I had a little trouble." Tim righted the chair across the table from Jacques and sat down. "The Dam was swarming with narcs last night. It was unreal. I thought I could spot them, you know. Like Wouter warned me. But there was one dude who kept flashing his cash—a real cowboy. Said he was from Albuquerque. Had the accent down to a T. When we finally got around to the buy, the jerk nailed me."

Jacques made no response except to extract a small leather book from his coat and make a notation.

"We were going over this bridge. Just me and a leather jacket in the back seat. The cowboy was driving. That's when I saw that my door was unlocked. The cowboy slowed down for this bakery truck, I kicked open the door and rolled out. By the time they'd stopped I'd jumped off the bridge." Tim rubbed his hand over his split lip. "Guess I hit bottom."

Jacques pushed his plate away toward the middle of the table and finally looked up. "And the police?"

"They pulled over. Looked around. But they didn't want to get wet. I dove under an old houseboat and hid between it and the wall until they took off."

Tim eyed the remains of Jacques' breakfast.

"Your account now totals 722 guilders," Jacques said, lighting a cigarette and exhaling a cloud of blue smoke. "I'm afraid I must charge you 250 for the lost merchandise."

"Charge the narcs," Tim snapped. "It wasn't my fault."

Jacques closed his journal and tucked it back in his pocket. "You have twenty-four hours, Tim. That should be enough time for you to cover last night's losses."

"You've already got my return plane ticket. That more than covers last night's stash. What can I do about it in a lousy twenty-four hours?"

"The ticket is collateral on your earlier loan." Jacques finished the remainder of his coffee. "That was our agreement. Do you really want me to cash it in? Is that what you want, Tim?"

"I need more time."

"And I need your passport, please."

"It's in my backpack." Fortunately he'd found his backpack in the park, right where he'd thrown it when the bakery man was chasing him.

Jacques motioned him to produce it. And as Tim fished it out of the bottom of his pack, Jacques told him, "With your looks, you can make fifty guilders a go for ten, maybe fifteen, minutes' work. Of course you'll have to put on some fresh clothes and shave. But then you've already had a bath. Last night, wasn't it?"

Tim reluctantly surrendered his passport, desperately trying to think of some alternative to propose.

Shaking his head in mock sadness, Jacques said, "I thought I'd made it very clear. I am not a charity for runaways." He pocketed Tim's passport. "I'll keep this for you along with the rest of your gear. Twenty-four hours.

"Or I'll be forced to see that the police get it. They won't be so tolerant. There will be serious problems for you getting back into the States." He took another drag on his cigarette and smiled. "I think Rembrandtsplein is your best opportunity."

Tim gagged. He might have thrown up, but there was no food in his stomach.

As Jacques pushed back his chair and stood, he placed a small packet of cocaine on the table. "In case you need a little help, Tim. Try telling them you've never done it before. They just might believe you. The price goes up!"

Tim picked up the coke packet as Jacques exited the cafe with Sprug in his wake. When he heard the yellow jeep roar to life and speed away, Tim reached for Jacques' plate and quickly crammed the last remnants of the soggy pancake into his mouth. And he tried very hard not to be sick.

# # #

When the doors opened at the end of the morning session, Raj pushed his way to the forefront of the departing delegates. His pockets full to overflowing with contraband fruit, an orange got away from him and rolled through the crowd. Deeply embarrassed, he chased it through the tangle of bodies.

Minutes later he ran through the neighborhoods he'd passed on his way to the Rai. He stopped at the corner where he'd encountered the young American just a couple of hours before. But the boy wasn't there.

Raj quickly scouted every street for three blocks around,

calling "Timothy!" and stopping a number of pedestrians to inquire if they'd seen an American youth with a blue backpack and a guitar. No one had.

After nearly an hour of searching, Raj gave up and dejectedly headed back to the conference center. He tried to hand out some of his fruit to the first people he encountered on the street. But no one accepted. And after one elderly woman darted across the street, through congested traffic to get away from him, he quit offering. As he ate one of the bananas for his own lunch, he vowed to carry the rest with him in case he met any other hungry strangers on the streets of Amsterdam.

# # #

Tim leaned close to the broken mirror hanging over a grimy sink in the employees' bathroom in the back of the Zeedijk cafe. Stripped to the waist, with a scrap of soap and maybe forty watts of dim light glowing from a naked bulb hanging high overhead, he was trying to shave with just the head of a disposable razor. The handle had broken off a week before.

He almost gave up. Not so much because of the rotten conditions, but because it was impossible to shave without looking at himself in the mirror.

CHAPTER 7

One by one the lighted signs blinked on all around Rembrandtsplein as Tim stood in the deepening shadows at the west end of the square. He watched the men and boys standing and smiling at passing cars from the curb of the plaza in the square's center.

Heavy metal rock music blasted from the doors of a nightclub advertising for customers as Tim finally crossed the street. For ten seconds he leaned against a lamppost at the corner of the plaza. Then, too wired to stand still, he backed away from the curb and bumped right into a boy about his own age. "Sorry," Tim said, hoping he didn't sound half as self-conscious as he felt.

The boy, dark-skinned with long jet-black hair framing a smiling, fine-featured face, seemed amused at Tim's obvious embarrassment. His eyes quickly took in Tim's freshly washed blue jeans and red sleeveless sweatshirt, as he offered his hand. "I'm Tibbe. I hope you're not going to stand here. I don't think I can compete with those boots."

Without a word Tim spun around and beat a hasty retreat, away from the curb, back toward a row of benches in the middle of the plaza. He couldn't go through with it. *There has to be another answer.*

# # #

A vast collage of faces filled the great expanse of Europahal as flagbearers from each country carried banner after banner through the aisles toward the towering platform constructed for the conference. To Raj, the music, the flags and the pageantry seemed like another, multicolored miracle. And he was to spend the next week here in Amsterdam—learning about evangelism, listening to evangelists, being challenged and equipped to go back home to India and fulfill his humble calling to preach in the back-country villages of northern India.

The music continued, the last of the national flags entered the back of the hall and a man stepped to the podium atop the platform far across the hall from where Raj and Abraham sat. The speaker was too far away to be seen clearly, but the gigantic screens looming up on each side of stage showed the picture of Billy Graham. And the voice booming out through the sound system high overhead was one familiar to audiences around the world. In the translation booths in the great auditorium, Dr. Graham's English words were simultaneously translated into more than a dozen different languages and beamed to headphones throughout the audience:

"Already more than 174 countries are represented here, and that is about ten countries more than have ever gathered for an event in the history of the world.

"I know many of you are weary from the long travels. Your minds and your bodies may feel as if they are in different places right now. But I believe that your hearts are here. And that's what counts.

"Now, an evangelist must be many things to many people. A preacher for this work must have the heart of a lion. The patience of a donkey. The wisdom of an elephant. The industry of an ant. And as many lives as a cat . . ."

#

Tim watched the action unfolding around him from the bench in the middle of the plaza. A man in an expensive, tailored suit, a European, maybe an American, Tim couldn't tell, sauntered through the square. He walked toward the curb and struck up a conversation with Tibbe. As they shook hands, Tibbe nodded and smiled at something the man said. Then the two of them began walking together, across the plaza, toward Tim. The boy seemed to be listening intently to whatever the man was saying, but as they passed a few paces away from Tim, Tibbe looked over, smiled, and inclined his head back toward the curb and the now-deserted lamppost.

A strange sensation came over Tim. On the one hand he felt like an observer, watching everything going on around him—a theatergoer seeing someone else's drama, someone else's life. Another part of him prodded him to move, to accept the reality and do what he had to do before it was too late. Yet another part of him, what felt like the biggest part, screamed out in protest against what the other parts saw and said he had to do. It was like three voices, three different people inside, all with different feelings and different personalities.

The stress was getting to Tim. Running away from home. The frustrating, fruitless search. Weeks of living on the streets, scrounging for food and a place to sleep. Maybe he wasn't completely rational. But he couldn't see any other answer. At least none that he wanted to consider.

Jacques had his passport and his ticket. He couldn't leave the country. He couldn't even leave the city without more money. He couldn't go to the police; he'd heard the horror stories about Americans arrested on drug charges in foreign countries. And after seeing Moira's horror story he knew he couldn't go back to Jacques without the money.

When Tim noticed two men across the street, making some kind of quick exchange, he remembered Jacques' little gift. *Maybe you'll need a little help.*

Glancing quickly around but seeing no one paying him any attention, Tim slipped the cocaine out of his pocket. After carefully making a tiny tear in one corner of the bag, he sprinkled a generous hit of the white powder on the back of his hand. Then he slowly raised his fist to his face and sniffed.

He coughed once as a numbing coldness burned slowly up his nose and back into his throat. A moment later he felt a rush, as if his heart shifted into overdrive and pumped blood, or something, rushing to the top of his head and into his brain. Rembrandtsplein came alive. The lights glowed brighter. The music, voices, and laughter echoed loudly in his head. And the sudden sensations flooded the uncertainty from his mind. The protesting voice inside him fell silent. And he knew he could do whatever he had to do to get home.

An accompanying surge of stand-up-and-move energy launched Tim to his feet. And his feet took him toward the curb.

#

Abraham Abimue sat on his bed, sorting through a pile of paper, when Raj opened the door and came out of the bathroom. The Indian wore only a pair of loose white linen shorts and a white hotel towel, wrapped around his head like a turban.

Holding up a tiny empty, plastic bottle, Raj said, "I poured this into the bath. It made the water green and full of bubbles."

Abraham shook his head and frowned. "Green water bad, brother. Brings sickness."

Raj frowned and walked to the telephone. "Yes, I would, please, request a moment with the hotel operator. Oh, good evening to you. This is Mr. Prasad speaking. I am honored to be your guest in Room 412 and I wish to thank you for the hot water that so generously filled my bath.

"I found this little bottle in the bathroom. But it seems to turn the water green. And I feared some kind of chemical . . ." He paused. "Oh . . . your kindness is most appreciated. A pleasant evening to you, too."

He replaced the receiver and turned to his roommate. "It seems it is a small gift from our hosts to make the bathing more pleasant."

"Still," Abraham said solemnly, "green water . . . very bad."

Raj frowned again. But when the African broke into laughter at this reaction, Raj realized he was being teased. He grinned sheepishly back at Abraham and shook his head, "The West."

Sitting on the edge of his bed, toweling his head dry, Raj watched Abraham organizing all the materials he'd collected on the first day of the conference. "We are like schoolboys again."

Abraham nodded and smiled. "I find many good messages here for my people."

"Your heart burns to preach?" Raj recognized and acknowledged their common bond.

"Oh, yes," Abraham nodded vigorously this time. "My heart burns. In my district, twenty-five churches I am pastor."

"You must not exaggerate too much, brother," Raj cautioned. "This can be a sin!"

Abraham laughed heartily at his young brother's reaction to his job description. "It is true, Rajam. Spirit of God convinces me twenty-five churches. It is good, yes? I stay two, sometimes three month in bush. One sermon for me good twenty-five times! When I come home, I am most welcome."

"You have a large family?" Raj asked.

Abraham's face brightened. "At home . . . one wife and

eight children wait for me. But I am asking God for motorbike. I ask long time now." He paused, looking thoughtful. "The day I do not walk . . . it takes four weeks only to serve all my churches. Then my family not have to wait so long."

Abraham sprang to his feet. Thoughts of home and family had brought the shy and quiet man to life:

"I tell you story, my friend . . . also most true. I once walking late at night, far out in bush." He strode across the room, acting out his trek. He stopped suddenly. "Lion there . . . just in front . . . facing on the way." He turned to Raj to explain: "Lions most wise when belly empty. One look straight at you this way, others circle back in tall grass." His arm swept behind him. "Then lion you see roars. Great fear comes to your heart!" He spun around. "You run back. Into many hungry jaws.

"But this time," Abraham resumed his story and his charade, "when this great lion roars . . . trees above my head shake their leaves. I close my eyes tight. And I pray. I stand still as a rock." He stood rigid in the middle of the hotel room. "I stand in the name of Jesus. I wait and wait. When finally my eyes open . . . hungry lion is gone!

"That is true story, brother!" Abraham said, taking a seat on his bed, and self-consciously shuffling through his conference materials once again.

Sensing his friend's embarrassment, Raj offered some reassurance. "I believe you, brother. Just like Daniel in the lions' den."

Abraham grinned, pleased by the comparison. "Lions Daniel face hungry, too. Most certainly." He turned his attention to a packet of small booklets, counted the stack, and then commented: "I am told all Gospel in this small book." He opened one, slowly turning the pages. "But many English words trouble for me."

"Shall we read it together?" Raj asked.

"Oh, yes, brother. Thank you." He handed a copy to Raj.

Raj flopped onto his stomach across his own bed, looked up at Abraham and indicated the cover title. He read, "Steps to Peace With God."

The African silently studied the cover and then opened the booklet to the first page and waited for Raj to lead him through:

"In all of life there is nothing more wonderful than discovering peace with God." Abraham interjected a sincere "Amen" and Raj continued to read. "Step #1 to this discovery is realizing God's plan. The Bible says . . . 'We have peace with God through our Lord Jesus Christ.'"

Abraham recognized a familiar passage: "'For God so loved the world that he gave his one and only son, that whoever believes in him shall not perish but have eternal life.'"

Raj turned the page and continued. "Step #2 . . . We must acknowledge our problem of separation. That God is holy and we are sinful."

"Oh, yes. That makes for our difficulty," Abraham interjected his own commentary.

"God did not make us robots to automatically love and obey him," Raj was reading again, "but he gave us a will of our own and the freedom of choice." Here he added his own personal comment: "Choosing our own way is separation from God."

Both men turned their pages together. And Abraham began to read, "Step #3 . . ."

When he faltered and looked to Raj, the young Indian continued: ". . . To recognize God's remedy—the cross. Jesus Christ is the only answer to this problem of separation. When Jesus Christ died on the cross and rose from the grave, he paid this penalty for sin and bridged the gap from God to all people everywhere."

From memory, Abraham recited the next words: "'God showed his love toward us, in that while we were yet sinners, Christ died for us.'"

#

The crowds enjoying the nightlife in and around Rembrandtsplein thinned a bit after midnight. But Raj had spotted two young Indians drinking coffee at a table of a sidewalk cafe just a couple of doors down from the entrance to the Schiller Hotel. He stood between them now, bending over and turning the pages of a small booklet as he read: "Step #4 . . . is making our response to God. We must trust Jesus and receive him as our Lord and Savior. Jesus said, 'Behold I stand at the door and knock; if any one hears my voice and opens the door, I will come in.'"

When he and Abraham had finished going through the booklet, back in their room, the African had turned off the lights, stretched out on the floor and gone to sleep. Raj was restless and wide awake. In the quiet darkness he had heard the street sounds far beneath his window. Not even Abraham's peaceful snoring could drown out their call.

Quietly he'd climbed out of bed, slipped into his clothes, and tiptoed out of the room. He'd walked twice around the square, averting his eyes from the revealing photos hanging in the windows of the topless bars, and handing out his supply of Christian tracts with such a friendly open manner that several people actually stopped and thumbed through the pages. Then he'd spotted the two university students who told him they were from Madras.

When one of them asked a question about the booklet he'd just finished sharing with them, Raj asked if he could sit down and explain. So he was busy pulling over a chair from a nearby table when the white Mercedes convertible rolled to a stop at the curb across the street. Raj never noticed the car. And he didn't see the American teenager in the red sweatshirt climb in and then slump down in the front seat as the car pulled back into the traffic and drove out of Rembrandtsplein.

CHAPTER *8*

Morning. Nearly seven according to Tim's watch, as he strode quickly through the streets of the barely stirring red-light district. Even as he walked he could feel his final snort of cocaine wearing off. His legs slowly turned to lead. His head ached with the concentrated effort it took not to think about the worst forty-eight hours of his life.

An attractively fresh young girl biked passed him and stopped a few yards ahead. "Hi, I'm Elly," she said as he approached.

When Tim ignored her overture and kept walking, she ran to catch up and push her bike along beside him. "You look like you could use a friend. Fifty guilders. You can tell me all about it. I'm in the mood to listen."

Tim glanced at the young prostitute without breaking stride. She didn't look more than sixteen. "You're out early, Elly."

She laughed. "Farm girl. Mornings are best. How about it?"

"No, thanks . . ."

She grinned and shrugged. "Okay. Your loss." Then she swung her leg over her seat and pedaled off with an undaunted, "Cheerio."

Jacques sat at his usual table. A waiter brought him an early breakfast and retreated into the kitchen as Tim stepped into the cafe. But the dealer didn't look up from his morning paper until Tim stood right in front of him.

"Tim . . . sit. How did you find the Rembrandtsplein?"

Tim pulled a large wad of guilders from his jeans and dropped them on the table. Jacques picked up the bills and made a quick, expert count. "Very good. I knew I could count on you, Tim. You have," he paused, smiling now, "integrity.

"Sit down, Tim," he insisted. "Have some coffee." He filled a cup and pushed it across the table.

"I'd like my passport and my gear back."

"Of course, Tim. That was our arrangement." The dealer snapped his fingers and Sprug disappeared into the kitchen to return seconds later with Tim's backpack and guitar. Jacques handed over the passport himself, saying, "That takes care of our losses from the other night. But, of course, there remains the matter of your previous debt. I believe that was 472 guilders."

Too drained to think, Tim couldn't manage a response before Jacques went on. "I suspect Rembrandtsplein is not your style, eh?" Tim said nothing. "Then there's only one other way for you to straighten out your situation."

Again he snapped his fingers and Sprug handed him a package wrapped in butcher's paper and tied up like a piece of meat. Jacques tore open the paper and placed a bulging bag of hashish on the table.

Tim wearily considered the options. Anything was better than Rembrandtsplein.

"The city is jumping with American kids, Tim. They have traveler's checks in their jeans. Get out there and make

the most of it. Just beware of narcs and cowboys from Albuquerque."

As Tim started to get up, Jacques slid another gram
packet of cocaine across the table. "An incentive. Because I
like you, Tim. You're a man of your word."

#

Raj and Abraham had finished another hotel breakfast
and were about to leave for the Rai Center when the young
Indian realized he'd left his official conference name tag up in
the room. He asked his friend to wait in the lobby while he ran
back up the stairs.

But as he walked down the long hallway of the fourth
floor, he saw the door to Room 412 had been left wide open.
Hurrying into the room, he jumped with surprise to find a
woman pulling the bedspread from his bed. "Goede morgen,
mijnheer," she said, glancing up.

Raj's first reaction, after the surprise, was that of chagrin; he assumed he hadn't made up his bed properly. But
Abraham's bed had been completely stripped and the African
hadn't ever used his. Then Raj noticed a stack of folded sheets
on the chair and immediately realized the woman must be
changing the bed linen.

"I'm afraid there's been some mistake, madame," he
said, hurrying across the room and gathering up the bedclothes
piled on the floor. "My friend and I are not yet leaving your
fine hotel. We are honored to be your guests another six
nights."

"Ik begrijp het niet," the woman replied with a shrug.
Then, muttering something else in Dutch, she snatched the
sheets from his hands and glared at him.

Realizing the woman didn't speak English, Raj rushed to
the phone and dialed the hotel operator. "This is Mr. Prasad,
your honored guest in Room 412. I'm afraid there has been a
misunderstanding. I have just returned to my room to find a

woman changing the bed linens." He paused to listen, a troubled look on his face. "But I am not certain my hosts, the International Conference for Itinerant Evangelists will pay for a maid . . ." Again he listened. "Even so, my friend and I are not leaving for another six nights and . . ." He shook his head at what he was hearing. "Oh! I am sorry to be troubling you."

The maid watched him curiously as he hung up. He smiled and nodded. Then he retrieved his identification tag and scurried out of the room. He would have to tell Abraham. But he already knew what the African would say: *The West.*

#

Tim stood fifth in line, easily blending into the curious collection of backpackers and drifters queued up in front of the general delivery window of Amsterdam's main post office. Like Central Station, there were always customers here.

The guy immediately in front of Tim in line, an American college kid with a backpack schlepped over one shoulder was looking straight ahead, but addressing Tim. "Guilders! I gotta unload some guilders."

Tim wouldn't agree. "Dollars, man. I'll only take dollars. You won't be sorry. This stuff is outrageous."

Finally conceding, the buyer surreptitiously slipped three bills back under the arm draped by the backpack. Tim accepted the money, noting the three familiar portraits of Alexander Hamilton. Then after a quick (and he hoped inconspicuous) look around, he tucked three dime bags of hash into an outside pocket of his customer's pack. It was his sixth sale of the day and it was not quite noon yet. He was getting the knack.

The cocaine helped. It'd been a day and a half since he slept, but with just a small hit every hour or so, he felt great. And the faster he could get rid of the hash, the faster he could get his ticket back from Jacques and finally skip the country. Nothing else mattered.

The line moved and as Tim nudged his guitar case along

the floor with his foot, he felt a tap on his shoulder. "Hi! Welcome to Amsterdam. I'm taking a survey." It was the blonde preppie from Central Station two days before. "I'm Sally. Remember?"

Tim looked around the post office. "Where's your friend, the snitch?"

"We had a fight. She insisted on the Hilton and I thought the lobby looked like a geriatric's ward. She left for Brussels this morning. How about doing the town?"

"What did you have in mind?" Tim was wary.

"I don't know. Maybe an afternoon at the Rijksmuseum and then one of those night rides on the canal. After that . . . whatever. I could use a guide who knows the territory."

"Ja! Mag ik je helpen?" The postal clerk spoke impatiently. It was Tim's turn at the window.

"Sorry. General Delivery? Tim Devon? D-E-V-O-N."

As the clerk walked to a wall of alphabetized pigeonholes, Tim turned his attention again to the blonde who said, "Devon? I can't think of any movie star named Devon."

"What movie star uses his real name?"

"Sir? Your letter?" The clerk was back.

Tim stared at the envelope on the counter. *A letter?* He'd only been going through the motions in the line to make his sale. He hadn't expected any mail.

"Is it from him?" Sally was talking again. "Not that I believe you've got a super-star dad."

The handwriting was Aimee's. She'd dotted the "i" in Tim with a heart.

"Hey, Devon. Did you go deaf?"

Tim picked up the letter and began walking toward the exit marked "Uitgang." Sally sprinted after him calling, "Hey, what about the museum?"

"Another time, okay? I just remembered an appointment." He was halfway down the outside steps to the street when the blonde called after him:

"What about tonight? The boat ride?"

Tim didn't even hear her.

Fifteen minutes later he sat alone on a canal wall, dangling his feet over the edge. A woman on a houseboat across the waterway was hanging wet shirts on a clothesline as he carefully tore open the envelope. He could almost hear Aimee's voice as he read her words:

Dear Tim,

I can't be sure you'll ever read this, but it keeps my hopes going just to try and find you this way. Your mom calls almost every day asking if I've heard anything. At least I don't have to lie.

A couple times she has cried. I could never picture your mom crying before; she was always so strong. But she loves you and she knows I love you and I guess it draws the two of us together.

Life is funny, huh? Is this what being an adult means?

I went to the library this week and checked out a stack of books about Holland. I looked at the photos and tried to picture you in them. I guess it made everything a little more real, but it also made me miss you more.

You've been gone a thousand years. And yet it seems like yesterday you took me to the beach and told me what you'd found out. What you had to do . . .

# # #

They're sitting on an outcropping of rocks. A warm Pacific breeze off the gentle surf blows a wisp of her long hair against his face. He holds her hand as he talks.

"I told her I needed to get all my papers and things in at UCLA. But she kept giving me this story, some bull, about misplacing my birth certificate. So yesterday, when I was downtown, I decided to stop at the Hall of Records myself.

"I waited in line for an hour while this civil service type at the counter dragged around and waited on the three people in front of me. A real smug jerk. It finally came my turn and I gave him my name. But he couldn't find it.

"I'm standing there like a fool. He's got the computer! And nothing would come up for DEVON on my birthday. It was

like the twilight zone. I'm getting irritated, figuring the guy is a complete incompetent. And he finally asks for Mom's maiden name.

"That's when it all spit out. She was there. My birthday. St. Francis Hospital. Father . . . 'BLANK'!

"The turkey gets this tight smile on his face when he tells me, 'That's how they used to do it when the mother chose not to name the father.'"

He pulls a folded computer copy out of his shirt pocket and hands it to Aimee. "Five bucks'll turn your life around."

He jumps down from his perch and walks along the wet sand at the edge of the water. After a couple minutes, Aimee catches up and slips her hand into his.

"It doesn't change who you are, Tim. Not to me."

"But I don't know who I am now. I grew up with a ghost for a father and a name my mother picked out of a hat. Now I find out my real father may be alive out there halfway around the world."

He stops and faces Aimee to tell her the rest. "I've got to try to find him. My mom doesn't know, but I'm leaving Sunday. I've got a reservation."

Tears begin running down Aimee's cheeks. "That's just three days."

"I know." He fights to hold his own emotions in check.

"But we had so many plans this summer. Your job . . ."

"I'm sorry."

"Me, too." She leans against him, her arms tight around his waist, her warm tears wetting his shirt. "What can I do?"

"Wait, I guess. If you want to. I have to do this, Aimee. I have to find out about me."

"Of course, I'll wait," she says looking up into his face.

And he bends down to kiss the tears.

CHAPTER 9

The Dutch insist that the changing North Sea tides flush out the canals of Amsterdam twice every day. But some of the flotsam bobbing against the canal wall below Tim's feet looked and smelled as if it had been there since the first canals were built in the 17th century.

Without really seeing it, Tim stared at the floating rubbish riding up and down on the gentle wake of a passing skiff. As the little boat motored on out of earshot, he reread the beginning of Aimee's letter. She went on to summarize the mundane details of her summer as if she were trying to make everything seem so normal. But her true feelings glared through again in the last paragraphs, in words it pained him to read:

After Gramps died, Gram once told me, "Absence makes the heart grow fonder." Now I know what she meant.

I know in my heart that you're alive out there somewhere. I just want to know you're okay. Please, if you're reading this . . . just a postcard. I won't tell anybody. And I'm always the first to check the mail.

Wherever you are, Tim, whatever is happening, please know much I care about you. And those feelings won't change, no matter what. My love, always, A.

# # #

Raj decided to skip the boxed lunch provided for the delegates at the Rai Center and take a walk instead. On the slim chance of finding the hungry American youth again, he hiked north toward the hotel and the street where the encounter had taken place.

When he reached the Singelgracht, Raj turned and followed the canal east toward its junction with the Amstel River. Just two blocks later he heard music, the distant strains of a guitar up ahead. A faint voice singing something sad in what sounded like English.

Hoping against hope, Raj sprinted out onto a bridge spanning the Singelgracht and scanned the banks of the canal far ahead. And there he was, sitting on the wall on the far side off the canal just a hundred meters away! Raj let out a joyous whoop of recognition and called out.

"Timothy! Timothy! Thanks God I found you this day!"

Tim changed keys, oblivious to the distant voice. When the sound of his own name finally registered, he looked up in surprise to see a dark-skinned stranger standing on the bridge waving furiously. A split second later he recognized the face and its 1,000-watt smile. *Yesterday. The lost Indian with no guilders for breakfast. But what now?*

"Hello again," Tim said, warily, as the Indian jogged to a breathless halt beside him. *What did this guy want now?*

Pausing to regain his wind, Raj grinned and answered the unspoken question. "I owe you a meal, Timothy. And truth be known, my own stomach would welcome an authentic Indian curry. I have had too many chicken sandwiches.

"Two Indian students told me of a place. We will find it. I am inviting you, brother."

Twenty minutes later Tim stood waiting just inside the door of a little cafe with the strange but descriptive name "Delhi Huis." The restaurant hadn't yet opened for the evening, but Raj had knocked loudly on the window until the owner came to the door. Leaving Tim to wait, the two had disappeared back into the kitchen.

As Tim noted the dozen or so tables, already set for dinner, loud, heated voices sounded from the kitchen. He couldn't understand a word of whatever Indian dialect Raj and the owner were using, but the tone was sharp. Like an argument. Pans clattered and crashed and Tim edged toward the door to make an unannounced exit.

But that very moment a beaming Raj stepped out from behind an ornately carved wooden partition and motioned for Tim to sit. "Please, any seat. You are most welcome."

For the next few minutes, while a lesser commotion continued back in the kitchen, Raj quickly told Tim why he happened to be in Amsterdam. How all his expenses had been paid to come to the International Conference for Itinerant Evangelists. "A major miracle from the kind hand of God," he said.

His wariness and suspicion slowly eroded by the infectious, open friendliness of his unexpected host, Tim found himself summarizing his own story for the Indian. And he explained his own reasons for being in Amsterdam. *A minor tragedy from the not-so-kind hand of fate,* he thought cynically, but he didn't say it.

Raj finally excused himself and disappeared again into the kitchen. Voices raised. And then he was back carrying a large tray heavily laden with a variety of dishes. As he placed them on the table in front of Tim, he explained what they were.

"Kabuli Channa. Aubergine Bhaji. Cucumbers and onions in yogurt. Very good. Vegetable curry . . . not too hot for you. Lime pickle chutney . . . my mother made me eat this during the rainy season to ward off sickness . . . full of vitamin

C. Basmati rice. Oh, and Shami kabab . . . ground lamb. . . most tasty."

He finally stopped and surveyed the table. "Is it enough?"

Tim laughed. And it felt good to laugh. "It's fantastic," he said, staring at the feast.

"So eat then, brother. I will join you in a moment. I forgot the chapati. It is bread," he explained as he headed back for the kitchen. "You will like it."

Tim dug in as once again he heard the voices from the kitchen. The owner shouted something that sounded like a threat. But Raj was back a moment later with the bread and went at the meal in typical Eastern fashion, eating, gesturing, and talking all at once.

"It is not stupid to search for your father," Raj said, taking up right where they had left off before he'd served the food. "Mine was lost to me many years ago."

Tim looked up from his plate. "He died, huh?"

Raj shook his head and shoveled in a mouthful of curry. "He lives this day. But I am no longer his son."

"How's that?"

"In India, there is the Hindu religion. Do you know of it?"

"A little. You wear turbans, right?"

"Sometimes," Raj laughed. "Not always. My parents were devout Hindus. It was my upbringing . . ." He paused as Tim gasped and grabbed for a glass of water. "The curry is too hot? Here, line your stomach with Papadou." He tore off a chunk of the bread and handed it to Tim. "Also have some of the yogurt, it cools the fire."

After Tim gulped down some of both, and nodded with relief, Raj continued. "When I was but twelve, they sent me to a nearby mission school. I was to be first in my family to be educated.

"My father dreamed that his son would one day be a

great Yoga. We were a poor family, but my meditation was strong. Many out-of-body experiences. Even as a young boy, I conversed with many spirits and traveled to distant worlds.

"When I went to school, my family warned me to ignore the Christian God. Christians were cow-eaters, you know? They had no respect for Karma. No understanding . . . very underdeveloped. I thought I was strong enough to resist, but the Lord Jesus captured my heart."

Tim forked in a mouthful of rice and chewed thoughtfully. "The missionaries worked you over."

"Very little was said," Raj responded. "It was perhaps the quality of their lives that made me curious. So in my third year, I borrowed a Bible without asking from the desk of my teacher. I reasoned there was nothing to fear. Lord Krishna offered me his protection.

"You see, Hindus spend all their lives struggling to get close to God. And in the Christian Bible I was astonished to learn that God wanted to get close to me. That he sent his Son to our planet to show us the way."

Raj paused to refill his plate and then pushed the aubergine bhaji across the table toward Tim. "My mother would be shamed to serve such a dish, but for Amsterdam . . ."

Tim shook his head. His plate was still half full, with his fourth serving. "Why couldn't you just believe whatever you wanted to? Keep it to yourself . . . avoid the hassle."

"When I experienced the love of Jesus . . . he warmed me in such a way it could not be a secret. People knew. And I longed to tell them.

"When my father heard, he declared me dead before the family. And only the heart of God was strong enough to receive my pain."

Sensing the sadness in the Indian's voice, Tim looked at him. "Your parents? You never saw them again?"

"As if I had not been born."

"Well," Tim said, after a long silence, "I've never seen

my dad." He'd meant it as an expression of empathy, but the moment he'd said it, he realized it sounded more like self-pity. As if his case was worse then Raj's.

The Indian didn't seem to notice. "I will help you look for your father, Timothy," he said. "Perhaps together we can succeed."

Tim smiled his thanks and shook his head. "I ran out of leads. My mother said his name was Di Bey. But I discovered that was an American variation. The only thing close in Dutch is Di Bie. And I called every Di Bie I could find in the book."

"Show me," Raj said, offering a pencil and watching as Tim wrote it out on his napkin—"Di Bie."

"But I've checked all the post offices. I've gone to the libraries. I've even gone to all the universities in Amsterdam. Nothing."

Raj stood and began gathering the empty dishes. "We need more tea," he observed. "Service is very bad here." And he exited to the kitchen.

Tim looked at the name written on the napkin and slowly retraced the letters with a tine of his fork.

They sit at the kitchen table, the Chinese take-out food, almost cold now, sitting unopened between them. Without looking up from his empty plate, he listens as she explains:

"We were students together at San Francisco State. Both seniors. Money was tight. He was there on a special international scholarship, I worked part-time. We finally decided to move in together and I found this little flat in the mission district . . ."

"In other words, you shacked up with him." Tim still didn't look up.

"It was the '60s, Tim. He was bright . . . he made me laugh. I think we loved each other. But it was clear to both of us that he would go back to Holland.

"Not long before graduation I found out I was pregnant. It didn't seem fair to Peter to ask him to change his plans. His

life was in Holland. And I wasn't about to try to trap him. So I never told him."

"How noble of you!" he says bitterly. "Carrying me . . . the bastard!"

"That's an ugly, stupid word! You were mine. And I've built a life for us."

"Why didn't you just get an abortion?"

She bites her lip and sighs, looking suddenly older than he's ever imagined her. "Because I didn't want to miss you, Tim. I loved you. I still do. And you've never given me any reason for regrets.

"I know I should have told you. But the time never seemed quite right to . . . I'm sorry. Can you, please, forgive me?"

He stands and walks out of the kitchen without answering. As he trudges back up the stairs to his room, he hears her crying and putting the uneaten supper in the refrigerator.

Tim jerked back to the present with a start. Raj was pouring him a hot cup of tea. It was probably a combination of things: three days with no real sleep; a bloated feeling rivaling any Thanksgiving afternoon he could remember; and coming off a twenty-four-hour cocaine high. But Tim felt as if he could doze off right there at the table.

Noting the obvious signs of exhaustion in his new friend, Raj fished a key from his pocket. "I am most fortunate, Timothy," he said, "to have at this moment a hotel room with two empty beds. My own business will keep me away for hours. Please . . ."

Tim eyed the key and then looked at Raj. "Why are you doing this?"

Raj merely shrugged and smiled. "The hotel people are most generous. I am certain it will please them if their lovely room is occupied. They are always tidying up. There is an abundance of hot water in the bath. Even a telephone."

Tim took the key. Hot water had never sounded so good.

He lay in the tub for almost an hour. Stirring only occasionally to run a little more hot water. When he finally climbed out and drained the tub, he took the opportunity to rinse out the dirty clothes from his pack and hung them around the bathroom to dry.

Sitting on the edge of Raj's bed, wrapped in a towel, he noticed the phone. *It would be so easy.* He glanced at the dialing instructions, picked up the receiver, and promptly hung up again. *Why not?* He at least owed his mother a call. She loved him. And he loved her. His initial anger had been prompted by his own surprise and hurt. He didn't even blame her now. Mostly he missed her.

He picked up the phone, gave the number he wanted to the overseas operator, and waited for the phone to ring in southern California where it was just 5:37 in the morning.

Three rings.

"Hello . . . who is this?"

He could tell he'd wakened her from a deep sleep. Her voice sounded groggy. But suddenly she was awake.

"Tim, is that you? Where are you calling from? Are you there, Tim? Please, Tim. Don't hang up, please . . ."

He couldn't do it. He couldn't bear to talk to her now. Not now, not after what he'd done. He'd hurt her enough already.

Gently, quietly he set the receiver back in its cradle. Then he pulled back the covers of Raj's bed, climbed in, and wearily closed his eyes. He felt too tired to think. And almost, but not quite, too tired to cry.

CHAPTER 10

The cook, who also owned the "Delhi Huis," lined up a row of cucumbers on his cutting board and attacked them with a meat cleaver that became a flashing blur. Seconds later he scraped an entire pile of uniformly sliced cucumbers into a bowl and turned his attention to Raj who stood at a sink piled high with dirty dishes.

Taking one look at Raj's sudsy water, the cook stormed over, brandishing the cleaver as he waved his arms in alarm. "Too much soap. Soap is very expensive."

Raj nodded and shrugged compliantly. But as the cook walked away, he asked the man, "How much do you pay your dishwasher when he is not sick?"

"Never mind," the man replied. "He is much faster than you. Tonight you must earn eighty-two guilders. You ate like a prince!"

"May I suggest a minor improvement in your Aubergine Bhaji?" Raj asked as the cook checked the temperature of his oven.

The cook turned and scowled. "Silence! I have work to do."

"The addition of ginger root," Raj advised. "Finely ground. My mother received much honor for her Aubergine Bhaji."

The cook slammed his cleaver down on his chopping block and glared at Raj, who suddenly devoted his full attention to scrubbing at a dirty dinner plate.

# # #

The door of the darkened hotel room opened slowly and Abraham Abimue slipped noiselessly into the room, determined not to wake his roommate who was already in bed asleep. He moved like a silent shadow into the bathroom and closed the door before turning on the light.

The African squinted as the brightness flooded the room to reveal two pairs of wet blue jeans, three t-shirts, and assorted socks and underwear draped over the tub, the towel racks and every other available protrusion in the room. He practically stumbled over the cowboy boots in the middle of the floor.

Puzzled, he flicked off the light and opened the bathroom door. Stepping over a backpack and a guitar case, he stalked catlike to Raj's bed. As he leaned over his sleeping roommate, Tim flopped over and Abraham stifled a gasp as he stared into a white stranger's face.

Just as quietly as he'd entered, Abraham retraced his steps to the door and opened it to check the room number. It was right. 412. But everything else was a mystery.

# # #

Every time Raj reached the bottom of a sink, a waiter carried in another stack of dirty dishes. Or the cook handed him a pan to scour.

Raj had long since stripped off his shirt and girded himself around the waist with towels. But he was drenched—partly from greasy wash water, but just as much from sweating in the kitchen's steamy heat. So to ease his discomfort and the growing fatigue, Raj began to sing:

"O for a thousand tongues to sing, my great Redeemer's praise . . ."

"Shut up!" The cook was waving his cleaver again. "I pay you to wash dishes, not as entertainer." He gestured to the front of the restaurant. "And my customers pay for my good food. Not for your bad singing."

At this reference to customers, Raj wiped his hands dry on his pants and walked to where he could peek around the partition and see the diners who now filled the restaurant. Returning to his sink, he grinned at the cook and exclaimed with an enthusiasm he didn't really feel, "Thanks God, your business is good tonight."

It would be a long night. Plunging his hands back into the sink, he began singing again, but softly this time, "O for a thousand tongues to sing . . ."

# # #

When Tim first opened his eyes, the surroundings made no sense. He was in a bed facing a wall with a window. His mouth felt dry, with a faint left-over taste of curry. *The Indian! Raj! The hotel room!*

He reached out and pulled on the tilt cord of the venetian blinds. The slats opened and light poured into the room. *Morning! How late is it?* His watch said 7:20. He'd slept for what? At least 15 hours.

He stood, yawning and stretching as he looked out the window over a deserted Rembrandtsplein. He almost jumped at the sound of snoring. He whirled around, but all he saw were two empty beds. His and the other which hadn't been slept in. Then, with the second rumbling snore, he spotted feet, on the floor, sticking out just beyond the other bed. Tiptoeing around the beds, he discovered a large black man, wearing a brightly striped robe, sleeping soundly on the floor with only an arm pillowing his head.

Tim first impulse was to sprint for the door, but he remembered all his gear. So he silently grabbed his pack and moved stealthily into the bathroom and closed the door. There he yanked on only a pair of damp jeans and his boots before stuffing the rest of his clothes down in his pack.

Slipping quickly and quietly back into the room, he snatched up his guitar and retreated cautiously toward the door. Never once taking his eyes off the sleeping black stranger, he felt behind his back for the doorknob, opened the door slowly and silently, and backed out into the hall. Glancing uncertainly at the number 412 on the door, he quickly finished dressing right there in the hallway. But his heart didn't stop pounding, nor did his breathing return to normal, until he'd passed through the lobby and exited the front doors of the Schiller Hotel.

# # #

Raj took the stairs two at a time all the way to the fourth floor. Then he hurried down the hall to his room and tried the door. It was locked. He knocked. "Timothy!"

He could hear someone approaching the door from the other side. And Abraham opened it.

"Good morning, brother!" the African greeted him. "I go now to the Rai Center."

"I will be with you in one moment. I must first change this shirt," Raj said, brushing by Abraham and stepping into the room. There was no sign of the young American, except for the slept-in bed.

Raj felt the curious eyes of his roommate watching him. Sensing that the African was too polite to ask, he explained, "I spent the night with friends."

"Hallelujah," Abraham beamed.

It seemed unnecessary to Raj, perhaps even immodest, to recount the wonderful meal he'd provided Timothy, or how he paid for it with his all-night labor. The Bible said much about doing charity for the love of God, not for the attention and praise of men. But on their way to the morning session of the conference, he did tell Abraham that the young man who had spent the night in their room was the same American who had begged him for food a couple days before. That brief explanation seemed to satisfy, and even please, Abraham.

It didn't do much to explain why Raj slept, conspicuously, through most of the morning session. Even at the close of the general assembly, when 8,000 evangelists stood and filled the great Europahal with a resounding hymn of praise, Raj remained slumped in his seat, sound asleep. But Abraham only smiled at his exhausted friend and whispered down the row, "Our dear brother spent the night welcoming friends."

# # #

Tim sat alone on the steps leading up to a locked, side door of the stately old cathedral ironically named "Nieuwe Kerk," Dutch for "new church." It was in fact built before Columbus sailed to America and only new in comparison to "Oude Kerk" which was built in the 1300s and still stood just a few blocks away at the edge of Amsterdam's red-light district.

A good night's sleep on a real bed, reinforced by a few periodic hits of the complimentary coke Jacques had given him, made Tim feel like a new man. Without moving as much as a block from the Dam, he'd found four good customers and sold all the hash he'd had with him. Tonight, once the nightlife crowds began to gather, he could easily move the remainder of his supply which was now stashed safely in a Central Station baggage locker with his pack and guitar.

Glancing around to be sure no one was watching, he checked his wallet and made a quick estimate without pulling out the wad of guilders. He'd had a very good day. With maybe two or three more like it, he could pay off Jacques and head back to California. To Aimee. And home.

There was no longer any reason to stay, he thought, as he carefully extracted the folded piece of paper from behind the money. He opened it, smoothed out the creases, and examined the page, torn from a 1968 college yearbook. Senior class photos. Two pictures circled in red. Peter De Bey and Janet Desmond.

Reluctantly he folded and tucked the page away again for safekeeping. Then, pocketing his wallet, he descended the steps and walked across the street, past the Koninklijk Paleis, the royal palace, toward the national monument on the Dam.

# # #

Raj decided to use the only free afternoon on the conference schedule in his hotel, catching up on his sleep. But when he wakened from a three-hour nap, his mind and his body felt restless. In the lobby he picked up a discarded tourist brochure showing a walking tour of Amsterdam. And with that he set out to explore the city.

From Rembrandtsplein it was just a short walk to Muntplein, a 15th-century square, facing the ancient mint tower where money was once coined. A few minutes later he stood looking up at the bronze statue of a grinning young street urchin, a favorite Amsterdam folk figure, in Spui Square.

Raj followed the walking tour route from there to a main thoroughfare heading north to the Dam. According to his brochure, when Amsterdam was first built, the Dam actually separated the Amstel River from the IJ, an arm of the Zuider Zee. It was now something of a national plaza spanning from the old royal palace to the monument itself, a seventy-two-foot white marble obelisk built after World War II as a national monument to those who had died. The people of Amsterdam assemble at the Dam for official events. The steps of the monument were also a favorite gathering place for international students touring Europe.

Walking briskly, less than a block from the Dam which he could see just ahead, Raj noticed a poster in a shop window and stopped in his tracks. The shop was a VVV office, an official national tourist information center, and the poster in the window, in bold English print, proclaimed an invitation for all interested foreign visitors to enroll in a special "MEET THE DUTCH" program.

When he'd read the entire poster, Raj hurried to the door and entered the office. The tourist clerk, a bookish-looking gentleman seated behind a large desk, looked up over the top of his half-frame reading glasses to inquire, "May I help you, sir?"

Raj approached the desk, smiling. "I was most pleased to be informed of your 'Meet the Dutch' program when I observed the sign in your window. Thanks God, my steps were directed to this very place."

The clerk stood and motioned Raj to a seat. "It has proven quite effective. Long friendships are sometimes established over a casual dinner." He reached to the end of his desk for an appropriate form as he asked, "May I know your name, please?"

Raj spelled it slowly as the man's pen scratched across the page.

"Thank you, Mr. Prasad. You are visiting from the great country of India and you would like to be a guest in a typical Dutch home. Very good!"

Raj smiled and nodded. "Oh, yes, thank you. His name is Di Bie."

The clerk suddenly frowned. "Sorry, Mr. Prasad?"

"Di Bie! Here I will write it for you." He leaned over the desk for the pen.

The clerk stiffened and rose to his feet. "Sir, it is quite impossible to request a specific individual. The program has a list of recommended homes willing to entertain foreign visitors. All invitations must be by mutual consent."

"But I am certain Mr. Di Bie will not deny me when he understands the purpose of my visit."

"Perhaps we do not share a common language," the clerk was becoming increasingly agitated. "I seem to be unable to express my . . ."

"Believe me," Raj interrupted, "I would not concern you if it was not of great importance." He sat in the chair in front of the desk, leaned forward, and lowered his voice. "You may tell Mr. Di Bie that the matter to be discussed happened during the time he lived in the United States. Perhaps eighteen to twenty years ago. How much time will you require?"

The man spun around and yanked a notebook off the shelf. Thumbing quickly through its pages he muttered to himself, "Di Bie. Di Bie. Di Bie."

Then he closed the book, shoved it back in place and turned to face Raj. "Di Bie is not on the list! And I seriously doubt it ever will be."

"And why is that?" Raj asked.

"If you can read, Mr. Prasad, let me suggest the telephone book!"

Raj smiled at the man. "None of the Di Bies were correct."

"Then," the clerk said sternly, "I am afraid I will be unable to help you, sir. Good day."

Raj took no offense. But he was not yet to be deterred. The uncooperative clerk was merely a temporary roadblock—a small bureaucratic cog in a bigger government agency. Glancing up at an upstairs balcony and a door with a name plate and title, Raj inquired, "Perhaps you could introduce me to the Manager-General of this office."

"Only by appointment, sir. The Manager-General is extremely busy during the summer tourist season."

Raj was about to request a time for an appointment

when something out the front window and across the street caught his eye. As he dashed to the door, he called back to the clerk, "Excuse me for your time!"

Seeing his salvation, the clerk hurried to the door as it swung shut. And he shoved the deadbolt into the lock. It was almost closing time anyway.

CHAPTER *11*

A t the monument Tim had overheard two backpackers talking about a cheap hostel that charged only six guilders a night. After he stopped them and asked for directions, he checked his watch. He could use a good place to sleep; he had the money to pay. Plus he had time to check the place out before evening business hours.

He'd walked less than a block when he heard a familiar voice calling, "Timothy! Timothy!"

When he stopped and turned around, there was Raj, darting across the street and running toward him. The guy seemed to be everywhere.

"You aren't following me, are you, Raj?" he asked good-naturedly as the Indian reached out to shake his hand.

Raj smiled and shook his head. "No, but perhaps God is directing my steps because I do have good news for you, Timothy. You will surely have help with your search now, brother. I have made my request known."

"To find my dad?" A faint hope flickered in his heart at

Raj's words, and then was doused as he listened to the account of the tourist bureau clerk. "Just forget it, Raj," he said when the Indian finished his story. "You've done enough for me already. I appreciate it, but I gotta go, I'm due over by Vondel Park."

"I can walk with you there," Raj said, matching Tim's pace. "My time is my own for another hour."

Tim decided it was simpler not to argue. If Raj wanted to come, it was okay by him. "I just have one question for you, Raj."

"Yes?"

"Who's the big black dude?"

"I don't understand."

"The man in the hotel room? When I woke up, I was afraid I was in wrong room."

Raj laughed. "So did he!" And when Raj told about Abraham's reaction at finding Tim in Raj's bed, Tim laughed, too. Raj went on to tell Tim a little about Abraham before he backtracked with the conversation by saying, "I can see that you have doubts, Timothy. But the tourist office may indeed be able to help you."

"Sure. Let's talk about the odds."

"Odds?" Raj sounded puzzled. "Oh, you speak of gambling. The stakes are most certainly high." He paused, as if thinking about what he intended to say. "But with God, there are no odds, only promises. And the Scriptures declare that the Lord is interested in everything that concerns us."

Tim couldn't help a cynical laugh. "Now, there's a mind for details. The world's pretty screwed up."

Raj stopped. "He is God," he said simply, as if that explained everything.

Tim never slowed his pace. Raj had to run to catch up. They walked in silence for a few minutes until they passed through the massive iron gate at the entrance of Vondel Park. But Tim had been thinking.

"Let's say there is a real God—like you say. If that were true, why wouldn't he just wipe out the competition? Set himself up?"

Raj grinned in surprise and pleasure at the question. "Timothy, you are a theologian!"

"Closest I ever got to any of that stuff was maybe singing 'Silent Night' at Christmas."

"Well, the God of the Bible chooses not to force himself upon us. It is his plan that we must each seek him for ourselves. But his love for us is so great that he sent his Son, Jesus, into the world to die in our place so that all who believe in him as their Lord and Savior will gain eternal life."

Tim knew the start of a sermon when he heard one. And he was in no mood. He broke stride and turned to Raj. "Look," he said, "I'm sorry. But I've gotta shove off."

The animation drained from Raj's face. Chagrin echoed between every word as he said, "I do not wish to remain silent, Timothy, when I should speak. And I do not wish to speak when I should remain silent. Only God is wise enough to keep me from this trouble. I am sorry."

He looked so suddenly despondent that Tim couldn't walk away. Raj had been too kind to him.

"Okay, just for the sake of argument, where would God get a Son?"

Raj brightened a bit, hesitated a moment, and then asked, "Could we not sit? I cannot respond to such a good question without thinking."

Knowing he was going to regret it, Tim shrugged his agreement. And Raj promptly walked to the edge of a small pond, where he stepped out of his sandals, sat on the grass, and casually swished his bare feet in the cool water.

As Tim drifted over and squatted on his haunches nearby, Raj began his answer. "The Scriptures say that 'before anything else existed, there was Christ, with God.' Perhaps Jesus called himself 'Son' because he knew it would help us understand that he was part of his Father. Just as we are part of our fathers here on earth.

"Jesus Christ, by his death and resurrection, became God's message to us. He became the Gospel. Mysterious sounding, yes! But, Timothy, I am here as witness to this truth. Even beyond history and outside the Bible, he is as real to me as any living person. And that is why I don't wish to argue about him. I only say, 'Seek him! Try him for yourself!' How else can you be sure?"

"You talk to him, huh?" This was more a statement than a question.

Raj smiled slightly and looked at Tim. "Oh, yes. A part of me is talking to him right now."

Tim had to smile. "Yeah? What does he say?"

Raj sloshed the water with his feet and was silent for a moment before he replied. "That he is glad we are friends."

Neither one of them said anything for a few seconds until Raj broke the silence. "Are you hungry, Timothy?"

Tim laughed. "I didn't think I'd be hungry for a week after yesterday. No, I had a good day. Made a few guilders. Can I buy you a chicken sandwich?"

Tim laughed again as Raj made a face and replied, "Thank you, but I plan to join with friends from the conference for a special evening meal." Then he went on to ask, "Tell me, what is your business?"

"I sell maps to tourists." It was the first thing that jumped to mind. "Guide them around. Help them take in the sights. Whatever they want."

Now Raj laughed. "You are a visitor who knows so much about this city? For sure, you are American! A true capitalist!"

Tim stood to his feet, determined to close the book on Raj now. And he felt better to be leaving him on a more positive note. "Thanks again for the great meal, Raj," he said, reaching down to shake hands. "For everything. I've really gotta get back to work now. Good luck, Raj."

"This is goodbye?" Raj stood.

"Can't spare any more time. But," Tim added as he backed steadily away. "if I ever get over to India, I'll be sure to look you up."

As Raj watched his new friend walk away, a very large part of him was silently praying, "You must help Timothy, Jesus. My words were weak."

# # #

Tim stood at the edge of deep midnight shadows outside a sprawling old warehouse on the river. The single light bulb burning above the door barely cast its meager light to where he stood behind a forklift, sprinkling a little line of cocaine on the back of his hand. He pocketed what looked like enough for one more hit and sniffed. Within a minute he knew he'd be ready to march through the door and sell the rest of his stash.

It hadn't been a good night. He'd spent almost four hours at the Leidseplein, after Rembrandtsplein, Amsterdam's second busiest nightspot. With two theaters, uncounted cafes, hotels, cabarets, and pubs, it offered everything from Shakespeare to striptease. But tonight it had also offered narcs. At least he'd thought he'd seen narcs. Maybe he was too wary because he'd come so far. But even with a of couple snorts of coke to bolster his courage, he hadn't managed to make even one sale. Every time he approached a likely customer, he felt someone was watching. So he'd finally given up and come here where he knew there'd be customers and where any narcs would be easier to see.

When Tim stepped through the warehouse door, he found the light wasn't much better inside. He could just make out a narrow path of bare wood between two long rows of sleeping bags spread on the floor. An occasional flicker of a flashlight revealed a pattern of heavy beams spanning the cob-webbed darkness overhead.

These backpackers didn't get much for their six guilders a

night. But then they were all probably on serious budgets. *I hope not too serious,* he thought, carefully picking his way through the building. A low babble of voices surrounded him. He could hear French, German, and he thought Italian. He listened for English. He heard a shriek of laughter behind him and the lonely lilting sound of a flute ahead.

He stopped beside a girl stretched out on top of her sleeping bag, reading a Stephen King novel by the light of a tiny battery-powered reading lamp. "Need something else to pass the night?" he asked. "You'll think you stumbled onto a cloud."

The girl turned the beam to shine on his boots and then directed it up his legs, across his chest, and into his face. "Hey!" he exclaimed, momentarily blinded by the beam. "You can just say no."

"No."

When he could make out a path again, he slowly moved on. "Hey, cowboy, over here." The voice came from the corner of the building where two guys sat on their sleeping bag, drinking beer and playing cards by the light of a small propane lantern. One was about Tim's age, the other maybe twenty-three. Both clean-cut, their blond hair and fair features indicated Scandinavian stock. If Tim had to place the accent, he'd have guessed Norwegian.

"I'm afraid this place stinks," the first guy, the younger one, apologized, as Tim dropped down to join them on the floor.

"I hear they hose it out every morning," Tim responded cheerily.

"The campsites were all full," said the second as he hospitably handed Tim an unopened can of cold beer. "What do you have? Something good?"

"Colombian. Best in this town."

The two guys had an exchange in their own language before the first one asked, "Is it cut?"

"I guarantee it. Wanna try a sample?"

Of course. We made a buy at the Dam yesterday. Cut so thin you couldn't get a buzz. We were cheated."

"Not by me. This is as clean as it gets around here. Mexico you'd do better. But that's a long way from home. And they aren't as friendly there."

As he talked, Tim pulled out a small bag of hash and scraped a little onto a tin saucer the second Norwegian slid toward him. Then he waited and watched as the other one pulled a pipe out of his pack and carefully dumped the contents of the saucer into the pipe bowl. His friend struck a match and a moment later a sweet pungent cloud enveloped Tim as his would-be customers passed the pipe back and forth.

"Okay," said the younger Scandinavian. "What's your price?"

"In guilders—a small bag for twenty-five. Large bag for fifty."

Tim saw them exchange looks before the second one said, "We were thinking of more. Can you supply in quantity? We leave tomorrow night."

His younger friend added: "We have long winter nights at home, you know? We want to be covered."

Tim felt his adrenaline kick in. He had fallen into a serious buy. Just maybe the answer to all his problems.

"What did you have in mind?" he asked, fighting to keep his voice cool.

"Could we get a volume discount if we paid maybe 5,000 guilders?"

"Sure, I guess so. But can you get in with that much?" Immediately Tim felt like kicking himself for raising the question.

"We've done it before. Can you connect for us?"

"Sure," Tim said, sounding as confident as he could. "No problem. What time tomorrow?"

A voice from the darkness, a girl's voice, interrupted the

moment: "You know there are rats here?"

A man replied, "And they all have two legs."

Unsure whether to read the voices as threats or friendly warnings, the older Norwegian whispered, "We should go outside."

"The narcs won't come here," Tim assured him. "It's okay." He didn't want anything to mess up this deal.

"It might be a slow night at the Dam," the guy said as he scrambled to his feet and picked his way through the maze of sleeping bags back to the door.

"Olf intends to be a famous doctor. And that makes him cautious by nature," the younger buyer explained in a whisper as the two of them stood to follow. "And we still have to set a meeting place."

Tim followed his cautious customers out into the night where the lone bulb above the doorway cast long lean shadows. But the older Norwegian, Olf, didn't stop there. He walked into the shadows around the corner of the building. Tim followed as the second buyer brought up the rear. Down a series of steps to a concrete landing next to the water.

"This should certainly be safe enough," Tim said.

"At least the air is better out here," Olf responded.

Tim was ready to complete their business. "You guys know the Rembrandtsplein? Let's say tomorrow about two? I'll be waiting by . . ."

The young guy behind him suddenly grabbed Tim around the neck, and Olf spun around to land a vicious punch to the solar plexus. Tim doubled over in agony and was instantly yanked upright and forced against a wall. A forearm shoved against the back of his neck pinned his face hard against the bricks.

Tim kicked back desperately as he felt another hand pulling the bulging billfold out of his pocket. But one of his assailants grabbed a handful of Tim's hair and banged his head into the wall. Again and again. One of them landed a sharp blow to his kidneys and Tim's body sagged against the wall.

But then the sensation of warm, wet blood running down his face from his head and his nose gave Tim a surge of strength. Enough to twist free and face his attackers. But not enough to stand against their combined charge.

Just as quickly as he'd broken free, Tim was flung to the ground and one of the Norwegians landed hard on top of him. A flurry of blows pummeled him about his ears and he felt a cold gray numbness creeping steadily up his neck, through the base of his skull and into his head. Three incredible lightning bolts of pain shot through his body from three swift kicks in his ribs, and everything went completely black.

The rain of fists and feet continued for half a minute after Tim's body went limp. Then Olf picked up Tim's wallet from where it had fallen during the scuffle. He whistled softly and swore in Norwegian as he pulled out the money and tossed the billfold aside.

Then he stood watch over Tim's motionless body for the five minutes it took for his friend to run back up to the hostel and gather their gear. When the younger thug returned, Olf nudged Tim with a foot and heard a faint moan.

"Let's go," his friend urged, handing over one of the backpacks.

Olf turned to walk away, and then stopped. Laughing, he bent down and yanked off Tim's cowboy boots, tucking them into the top of his own pack before he ran off into the night.

CHAPTER *12*

Faint streaks of light in the eastern sky, the first gray fingers of dawn, pushed back the night over Amsterdam as an early morning barge plowed north along the far bank of the Amstel. The distant drone of the ship's diesel engines carried clearly across the river, prodding Tim out of a bottomless blackness into the dense fog of semi-consciousness.

The haze slowly dissipated from his mind, only to be replaced by penetrating cold and pain. With effort, he forced open the one eye that wasn't swollen shut and tried to focus. Where was he? He raised his head and the gray world of shadows began to swim and spin. He opened his lips in an involuntary moan and felt the dried river of blood loosen and crack.

Ten minutes passed before he sat up and steadied his throbbing head against his knee and remembered where he was. *The hostel. The two Norwegians. The big buy. His money.*

His billfold was a dark blur on the ground fewer than three feet way. *Empty!* The sudden images that flashed through his mind—Moira's eyes, her flailing arms, Jacques' face—were crystal clear.

He had to get away.

As he maneuvered himself to his knees, he spotted the folded page from the old yearbook, lying on the ground where it had fallen when his muggers discarded his empty billfold. He picked it up and jammed it into his pocket as he struggled to a standing position.

He only had one place he could go. The Schiller Hotel wasn't far. Just a few blocks. If he could walk.

Tediously, he began to trudge along the river, toward a gate in a high fence, and the street he could see just beyond. But he'd only taken a few steps when a large piece of gravel sent a new pain through the bottom of his foot. It was only then that he looked down and saw that his boots were gone.

And he wondered if he would ever see California again.

# # #

Raj walked purposefully from his hotel and started on the now familiar trek to the Rai Center. He wished to arrive early this morning in order to have time to browse through the many displays. He had never known there were so many ministries, so many Christian organizations working around the world. He had already picked up many helpful printed materials. But he found inspiration just walking among the booths.

Raj had only walked about a block and a half along the quiet morning streets when he suddenly stopped and listened. He thought he'd heard his name.

About to decide he'd been dreaming, he heard it again.

"Raj . . ."

He turned around but saw no one.

"Raj . . . over here, . . . been waiting for you."

Then he saw him, lying between a bicycle rack and the building. "Timothy?"

Blood crusted over a long gash in Tim's forehead and between his nose and lips. One side of his face had swollen his eye completely closed. "Brother, what has happened to you?"

Tim's babbling sounded incoherent to Raj: "Have to hide . . . He'll get me . . . I'll be dead. Like Moira . . . have to hide."

Raj carefully lifted Tim's shoulders and leaned him gently against the wall. "Your beautiful boots!"

"They jumped me. All the money's gone!"

"Were there six this time?"

"Two guys . . ."

"We must contact the police to . . ."

"No police. He'll find me. I'm dead."

"Timothy, you are alive, thanks God! Did they take your guitar also?"

Tim shook his head. "It's locked up at the station."

"Someone is searching for you?"

Tim slumped to the side, trying to lie down again. "Forget it."

Raj pulled him upright again and said with a brief flash of temper, "You call to me and now I should forget it? I won't!"

Then, draping Tim's left arm over his shoulder, Raj boosted him to his feet and pulled his room key out of his trousers. "Here . . . you will be safe at the hotel. I will return at the first possible moment."

He watched the boy take a few steps and called out to him. As Tim stopped and leaned against the building for support, Raj stepped out of his sandals. "An Indian can go barefoot on the streets. It is expected. No one will notice." He slipped the sandals onto Tim's feet.

"It's only two blocks to the hotel from here. Can you make it?" he asked as he stood back up.

"I think so. I've been lying here for an hour and I feel a lot stronger."

Raj stood and watched his friend walk back toward the Rembrandtsplein. Tim would make it.

#

The hand-lettered sign on the door bore the name of the Christian relief agency: "The Samaritan's Purse." Raj pushed the door open and walked into a large Rai Center room that looked just like what it was—a clothing distribution center.

The only person was a gray-haired woman, her back turned, working behind a counter at the far end of the room. When she finally heard Raj and turned around, he was standing at the counter.

"Well, hello!" she beamed in an American, deep-southern drawl.

Raj bowed in greeting. "Good morning to you, dear sister."

"I'm afraid nobody's around yet. I'm just a volunteer, here to help with the sorting. Anything I can do? Maybe answer any questions for you?"

"I was told that 'Samaritan's Purse' is providing clothing for those attending the conference where the need is great."

The woman nodded enthusiastically. "We're especially trying to help those evangelists from Third World countries. You know, those from remote places where shopping is a problem."

"And money," Raj added with a smile.

"That too," she conceded. "Anyway, we are open every day right after lunch."

"I assume I am Third World. I keep hearing this. Although how we achieved this position is not clear to me." Raj paused, then decided to press his case. "I am hoping to be blessed with shoes!"

"Fine," the woman replied. "You come back after lunch and we'll fix you up."

Raj bowed again and backed away. When he turned and the woman saw him padding across the floor in his bare feet, he heard her exclaim, "Mercy!" And then she was rushing after him.

"Maybe you should come back here!" She took his arm and led him to a long row of tables strewn with row after row of shoes. Babies' shoes. Children's sneakers in a rainbow of colors. Women's shoes, from dressy to rain boots. The men's styles were more limited. "They're all new," she explained. "But kind of picked over. What size do you wear?"

"Whatever you are kind enough to share with me?"

"Well, they have to more or less fit. But you can try anything on these tables."

Raj deferred to her. "The gift is from the Samaritan's Purse. It must be of your choosing."

"Mercy," she muttered, momentarily flustered by this clash between Eastern and Western cultures. Then she looked at Raj's feet and moved to the nearest table. "Well, since you don't know your size . . ." she picked up a pair of heavy brogans. "Here! Will these do?" she asked, handing them to Raj.

He smiled wide to mask a grimace and forced his feet into the high-topped leather work boots. Not exactly a tropical or summer item. The length felt about right, but they were extremely narrow.

The woman frowned. "Don't they pinch a little?"

"My feet are insignificant—but somewhat wide," he assured her. "This condition comes from not wearing shoes until I was ten. Surely they will stretch. They are God's gift to me this day." He stood and walked around to show they were okay.

The volunteer smiled her pleasure and quoted a Bible verse, "'Blessed are the feet of those who preach the gospel.'"

Raj bowed in gratitude and moved toward the door, struggling not to limp.

# # #

Tim hurried across the hotel lobby. Even so, his appearance drew several curious stares and one genuine gasp before the elevator doors slid closed and he leaned against the side of the car to brace himself for the upward movement. The fourth floor hallway seemed a lot longer than it had been. So by the time he let himself into 412, he barely made it to Raj's bed to collapse. Some time later he awakened enough to stumble to the bathroom.

He almost gasped himself when he looked in the mirror. But ten minutes with a hot wet washcloth greatly improved his appearance. The cuts on his face and the bloody nose were fairly minor. The bigger damage, the real pain, concentrated in the hard swollen knot behind his right ear, and in the ribs. He felt, but couldn't see the lump on his head. It could be a concussion. Then he pulled up his shirt to discover one ugly black bruise stretching from his hip to his armpit. He gently probed at the edge of the discoloration. Once was enough. When the pain subsided, he walked gingerly back to the bed and eased himself down on his other side.

# # #

Raj came back to the room at noon to find Tim sleeping peacefully. Tim looked so much better with his face cleaned up, that Raj felt reassured enough to return to the conference without waking him. He knew the shock had worn off and Tim's body needed all the sleep it could get to recover from its damage. Besides, Raj had been devising a plan. And he needed help to put it in motion.

# # #

The tourist clerk stood at the window, straightening the pamphlets on a shelf when he looked across the street and saw them. His first instinct might have been to rush to the door and lock up for the afternoon, but two British women were already in the office, looking at rail and ferry schedules.

There was nothing to be done but to stand his ground and hope they weren't all heading his way. Maybe none of them were. They were stopped. What were they doing? Praying?

They were coming now, right across the street.

Raj was leading the way, limping as fast as he could into the tourist office. Crowding in behind him were Abraham Abimue and one of his friends—a towering Masai warrior carrying a ceremonial shield and a spear. He was flanked by an elderly Indian woman wearing a brilliant orange sari and a Korean in a gray Western business suit. Pushing into the office behind them was a young Guatemalan woman in a blue poncho.

"Greetings again, my friend," Raj said, bowing and smiling at the clerk. "My friends and I have come personally to thank the Manager-General of the VVV for opening the great city of Amsterdam to the International Conference for Itinerant Evangelists."

The group members smiled and nodded agreement as the two British tourists stared in surprise. But the clerk remained determined. "But, sir, I explained about the appointment . . ."

Raj was not to be stopped. He smiled and indicated the tallest member of the delegation. "This brother here is a former chief of the Masai in Kenya. He has personally killed three lions . . ." Turning to the warrior, he asked, "Brother, was this the very spear?"

The dignified black man nodded solemnly and extended his weapon.

Turning back to the clerk, Raj continued. "Perhaps you would like him to demonstrate how this great feat was accomplished? Of course, there are no lions here, but he has a good imagination."

"No demonstrations! Please!" Then, with a sigh of resignation, the clerk acknowledged defeat by reaching for the phone to buzz the upstairs office.

CHAPTER 13

The Manager-General opened her door to welcome the entire delegation. She was a tall, brown-haired Dutch woman, professionally dressed in a blue suit. Conditioned by years in the public relations business, she seemed more intrigued than put off by the intrusion of this unusual group of visitors. She shook everyone's hand and graciously accepted their thanks on behalf of the city for hosting the Amsterdam 86 convention.

Then, seeing no one making a move to exit her office, and suspecting an ulterior motive for the visit, she smiled warmly and asked, "Is there anything else my office can do to make your visit here more profitable?"

Raj seized the opening and related Tim's story as he knew it. And the Manager-General sat at her desk listening attentively to everything he said. When he concluded, she remained silent for a time, her fingertips pressed together, her facial expression intent and thoughtful.

"A troubled young man's soul hangs in the balance," Raj

added.

"Di Bie . . . twenty years ago. You're not offering much in the way of clues."

Raj nodded and shrugged slightly, conceding the point. "We are entirely in need of your help."

She looked up at the faces gathered in front of her desk and smiled reassuringly. "I will be in touch with friends at The Hague. Perhaps some office there will have records of exchange students who went to the United States during that period. I don't know what else to do."

She stood to shake hands again all around and added, "I must tell you I have followed your conference with great personal interest. Perhaps because I join you in your faith!"

At that, a resounding chorus of "Hallelujahs" echoed off the office walls. And a worried clerk bounded up the stairs to check on the safety of his superior, only to be embraced warmly by one smiling foreigner after another as they streamed out of the Manager-General's office.

# # #

Tim sat in hot water up to his armpits, a cup of steaming coffee on the edge of the tub. He'd been there a half hour before Raj and Abraham had returned from the evening session of the conference and almost an hour since. And the bone-shaking chills that had plagued him since late afternoon were finally subsiding. Soaking in the warmth eased the aching and reduced the pain in his side to a dull throb.

But the water that soothed his body was doing nothing to soothe his mind. As the physical pain receded, he was forced to deal with his fear, his feelings. A severe depression, typical after traumatic injuries, intensified the despair. And that was multiplied by his abrupt withdrawal after forty-eight hours of intensive cocaine use.

Everything was crashing down around him. There was no escape. And no way to fight. It was over. He'd never make it home again. And the pain of that thought brought him closer to screams than the agony in his ribs. And he realized he was now sweating profusely.

"It's too hot in here," he complained. "This dump claims to be first-class? It's a joke. I need a bucket of ice."

Raj stood at the sink, shaving with a straight-edge razor that looked like a weapon. He looked down and met Tim's glare. "They just brought you the coffee, Timothy."

"Now I need ice!" Tim twisted the cold faucet wide open and thrust his head under the gushing water.

Troubled, Raj set down his razor. "I have asked the Lord to help you."

Tim grunted in disgust. "You really want to do something? What I need are some pills . . . for the pain."

"The hotel operator informs me that she can call a doctor."

"He won't do anything!" Tim paused and his tone changed from belligerence to pleading. "There's this guy that sells them on the Dam. His name is Wouter. Give him thirty-five guilders. For the red capsules. Just tell him it's for me. Please, Raj!"

"I do not possess thirty-five guilders. Timothy, will you pray with me?" he dropped to his knees beside the tub. "The Lord is a very present help in our times of trouble."

"Then get him to shovel thirty-five guilders my way!" Tim snapped. "Go on! You're so tight with him. Cash in some chips!"

Raj stood again. "I will bring ice, brother," he said back over his shoulder as he walked from the room.

"Just forget it!" Tim yelled afte him "I called your bluff, man! So just forget it!"

# # #

He's standing at the curb with Tibbe, smiling at the passing traffic. A man in a Mercedes convertible stops and motions them both to get in. As the car pulls slowly around the square, thousands of people lining the sidewalks turn and stare at him. And then he hears someone scream his name. He looks back and sees Aimee and his mother running out of the Schiller Hotel calling after him. But the car won't stop. Suddenly he's on a rooftop watching Jacques shooting heroin into the arm of a blonde girl. The girl turns. It's Aimee. She looks at him with tears running down her face and she asks, "What am I supposed to do?" He calls to her, but she doesn't hear him. She's waving her arms like a bird and flitting around the rooftop. Then she steps off the edge, turning in the air to wave goodbye as she plunges out of sight. He screams her name. Jacques and Sprug begin to laugh as he runs to the edge and jumps. And then he's falling down, down, down, toward two bodies splayed out on the ground below. One is a black woman in an orange dress. The other is a girl with long blonde hair. He's falling right on them and he screams.

Tim jerked upright on the bed, shaking with the terror.

The scream awakened Raj who sat up where he was sleeping in Abraham's bed and looked across the darkened room. "It was just a nightmare, Timothy. Try to go back to sleep. Everything will be all right in the morning."

Without saying a word in reply, Tim eased himself back onto his pillow. But he couldn't go back to sleep. It wasn't just a nightmare. Everything wouldn't be all right in the morning. Things would never be right again. Ever.

# # #

Raj, with Abraham at his side, walked briskly toward the Rai Center for their morning session. The boots still felt heavy, as if he were sludging through a muddy back-country road in rainy season. But his feet had room to breathe where he had cut holes at the toe and the sides with his razor. He realized the shoes looked a little strange, but he no longer had to limp.

The two evangelists scurried across a busy intersection

and again slowed to a fast walk. "In my country," Raj said to his friend, "a spiritual path . . . it is most honorable. Not the same here . . . in the West."

"No," Abraham agreed. "But people same. Pride and sin build high wall of stones. Jesus waits . . . on other side for us."

Raj considered Abraham's words for a time before he replied. "I think perhaps Timothy does not need to be made to feel guilty. He carries more of that dark burden now than he can carry."

Abraham nodded thoughtfully. "Sin like heavy stone on heart. Only cross of Christ can lift this sadness."

The two men crossed another street and Raj stopped on the sidewalk outside the Rai Center. "I would lead him to that place of rest, brother. But I cannot make him stay."

Abraham laid a comforting arm across his friend's shoulders and said, "Only God can do more."

But Raj couldn't shake his own heavy feeling of failure. *Such good news! Why wouldn't Timothy listen?* "Perhaps I have misunderstood my calling," he lamented, trudging into the building.

# # #

Tim tried to sprint across the Rembrandtsplein. But it was more like a jog—what with his pack on his back, the guitar case clutched in his hand, and the agonizing pain in his side. At any moment, until he ducked into the safety of the Schiller lobby, he expected to hear his name shouted out or the screeching of the brakes of a jeep.

He'd made it without being spotted. Through the crowds to the lockers at Central Station. And back to the hotel.

After depositing his belongings on Raj's bed, he made a quick search of the hotel room to find the complimentary stationery. Raj had left a pen on the nightstand.

For an hour he wrote, pausing only periodically to carefully compose his thoughts. The words poured out, filling four pages, front and back. Then he was done. He reread it once, folded the pages, and slipped them into one of the hotel envelopes. He sealed the flap and addressed it from memory.

Propping the letter on the bed, against the guitar case, he retreated to the bathroom. At the sink he jammed on the cold faucet and bent to inhale the water. His mouth felt so dry. A few seconds later, his thirst quenched, he lifted his dripping face and studied himself in the mirror. Rivulets of water ran down over his swollen features and dripped off his chin.

Her face. Aimee's face. Her tears run down. Just an arm's reach away. The surf swashes around their feet. And she says, "What am I supposed to do?"

"Wait, I guess," he's saying. "If you want to. I have to find out about me."

He stared at the mirror. At his face. Knowing and hating what he'd found out. Never wanting her to know . . .

He turned to walk back into the room and hastily scratched out another note. When he finished, he carefully placed the first note inside his guitar case and closed it again before he laid the second note on top of the case. Picking up his pack, he felt the change in his pocket, judging he had enough coins left for his purpose. Then he looked around the room once and walked to the door. It clicked once and locked as he pulled it closed behind him and walked determinedly down the hall.

CHAPTER 14

The summer sun shining through the plate-glass window warmed Raj where he sat on the floor of an outer corridor of the Rai Center. Seated with his back against a concrete support pillar, he faced the window. But his eyes were closed, his chin resting on his knees which he hugged to his chest. The sound of music drifting from the Europahal drowned out his voice as he prayed aloud, softly.

"Oh, Lord, I know You do not fail if I am not effective. Forgive me for placing too much value on my own words."

The music stopped and someone began to speak before Raj finally stood. But instead of rejoining the throng of his fellow evangelists in the great hall, he descended the escalator and left the convention center, walking as fast as he could toward his hotel.

# # #

When the metrotrain shot up out of the tunnel, the sudden burst into sunlight forced Tim momentarily to shield his eyes.

Slowly opening them again, he was struck by the shiny-clean sheen on the seats, walls and windows of the sleek new passenger car.

He knew he was going to leave a smudge on the glass where he leaned his head against the window. But he didn't care. He was almost oblivious to the other passengers in the car, except to note with satisfaction that fewer and fewer remained after each stop. With any luck, he'd be the last one out of this commuter train at the end of the line.

# # #

Raj twisted the key in the lock and burst into the hotel room. "Timothy, how . . ."

He stopped when he saw the guitar on his bed. He snatched up the note to read:

This crazy guitar is in my way for the last time. You keep it now, Raj. And when you play it, remember the guy who tried to hustle you for breakfast . . . Tim Devon.

P.S. There's a letter in the case. I'd like you to mail it before you leave Amsterdam. Thanks.

Raj opened the case and picked up the letter. It was addressed to "Miss Aimee Lynn Rasmussen" in some California town he'd never heard of. As he returned the letter to the case, a dark sense of foreboding swept over him.

He jumped at the sudden jangling of the phone.

"Yes, hello," he said into the receiver. "This is Mr. Prasad."

"I think we have found your Mr. Di Bie."

In the moment it took him to place the Manager-General's voice, her words failed to register. "Excuse me, please . . ."

"Mr. Prasad, I have an address for you. For Mr. Di Bie. Are you there?"

"Oh, yes," he exclaimed. "I am here Mrs. Manager-General!"

Sixty seconds later he had fled his room, descended four flights of stairs, crossed the lobby, and had hit the sidewalk in front of the Schiller Hotel in a full run. He was halfway across the Rembrandtsplein when he stopped dead in his tracks. He had no idea where to go.

# # #

When the train glided to a stop at a lonely metro platform on the farthest perimeter of Amsterdam, Tim decided he'd gone far enough. One other passenger disembarked at the Bijmer Station. Tim, pretending to wait for another train, took a seat on a bench and watched as the man left the platform and crossed over the tracks to a long bicycle rack. After what seemed like an eternity, the commuter unlocked his bike and pedaled off toward a village Tim could just make out in the distance to the west of the tracks.

He was finally alone.

# # #

Raj remembered Tim mentioning a man on the Dam. It was as logical a place to start as any. But Tim could be anywhere in the afternoon crowds.

Raj quickly circled the monument once and then sprinted to the top step for a better view across the square. *Dear God, if You are counting the hairs on his head right now, please show me his face.* Nothing. Only a sea of faces.

Running down the steps, Raj dodged a tram and ran up the Damrak toward Central Station.

# # #

Tim crossed the platform from the metro side to the other. Two transcontinental tracks ran alongside the metro, but the fast express trains made no stops at Bijmer Station. He'd checked the schedule to be sure.

He stepped across the yellow safety line to the edge of the

platform and looked down at the tracks. At a joint, where two rails came together, it looked as if one was a fraction of an inch higher than the other and he wondered for a moment how much of a difference it took to cause a derailment.

He heard the train before he could see it. *Did the steel tracks somehow transmit the sound?* His mind seemed stuck on trivial musings.

He looked to the north and saw the faint light of the train's headlight growing steadily brighter. Bigger. He inched to the very edge of the platform and looked down at the tracks. It might have been his imagination, but as he stared at the top of the rails where they'd been worn shiny by countless steel wheels, the track itself seemed to shiver.

He stole a quick look up the tracks to see the diesel engine of the train barreling toward him. He looked back at the tracks. They were definitely vibrating now, like a giant, rumbling, tuning fork drawing him down, down, down.

CHAPTER 15

But instead of falling forward onto the rails and under the grinding steel wheels, he sagged backward and dropped hard to the concrete surface of the railway platform. The jolt to his ribs forced a scream through his lips but the cry was instantly smothered by the buffeting wind and the rolling thunder passing in a blur just three feet from his head.

Finally the train was gone. Even the tracks were still. And he could hear the quiet sound of his own, dry, racking sobs. The physical pain was bad enough. But what tortured him far more was the agonizing realization of a terrible truth: as much as he wanted to die, his will to live was stronger.

Death would have been so easy. So quick. So definite. Living meant only pain and questions. And then death.

But Tim's will to live, once exerted and accepted, quickly gained strength. It forced him to his feet. And as he caught the next train back to Amsterdam, it forced him to think. About surviving. And about how to do it.

#

Raj circled the big duck pond in Vondel Park at an agitated pace. He stopped and described Tim to a cluster of backpackers sitting and reclining in the grass. But all he got in response were shaking heads and shrugs.

He stopped an elderly man carrying a cane and walking a little dog—a fat, elongated creature resembling an overstuffed sausage. As Raj described Tim, the dachshund sniffed suspiciously around his self-styled shoes like a critical cobbler. The man couldn't help either.

Raj finally exited through the park's main gate. He had to keep looking. *But where?*

#

The young German stood at the window of a street corner canteen, half a block from Rembrandtsplein, when Tim spotted him from across the street.

"Hey! Wouter! Been looking for you!" Tim crossed over as the traffic cleared.

Wouter turned to face him with a can of beer in one hand and a bratwurst in the other. "Yeah?" He looked up and gestured for Tim to follow him as he headed for the nearest curb. There he sat and began to eat his late lunch.

"You look like a tram hit you," he muttered through a mouthful of bread and brat.

Tim got right to the point. "I need something, Wouter. Gotta get kicked up," he said. "Just a couple uppers."

Wouter took a long sip of beer and looked at Tim. "What are you on?"

"I'm just sick, man."

"You're crashin'."

"I'm just hurt and sick. That's all. But I need something, some help to get my head straight."

Wouter turned back to his food. "You're a risk now. Jacques is looking for you."

Tim tried not to let his voice waver. "I'll see him. I know I have to. But not like this. You gotta help me."

"What kind of cash you got?"

"Just carry me for a few hours. I'll make good."

"Rip off some clothes. Get me a couple of pairs of jeans. Something I can turn over fast."

"I'll give you my watch to hold." Tim slipped it off. "Collateral."

"Used," Wouter said, stuffing the last bite of his bratwurst into his mouth.

"Don't give me that crap!" Tim struggled to his feet and angrily faced the German. "I got it for graduation. Worth at least 200 bucks! Only had it for two months."

"You yelling at me?" Wouter stared coldly up at him.

Tim quickly slumped again to the curb. "No."

He handed over his watch. Wouter took it and pocketed it without an appraisal. Then Wouter held out his hand with a small amphetamine capsule in his palm. One end was red, the other clear with tiny white beads inside.

"It'll bring you up for a couple hours. Work the metro station over by Waterlooplein. Snatch some purses. If you're not back by four, I go to Jacques."

Tim popped the pill and downed it with the last swallow of Wouter's beer. Then he stood again and walked off down the street.

"I don't want your watch," Wouter called after him. But Tim just kept walking.

# # #

The yellow jeep, its canvas top off for the afternoon sunshine, practically blocked the narrow street. But Sprug sat immobile behind the wheel, ignoring the insistent horn and the angry complaint from the driver of the green sedan that finally swung out and eased around by running up onto the far curb.

Eventually Jacques appeared on the sidewalk, exiting

from a door under a sign advertising "Adult Books." And Sprug leaned over to unlatch the door. There was a shout and Wouter came running up the sidewalk from behind.

"Just saw the kid," he reported. "He's begging me for a fix. So I got him working the metro over by Waterlooplein." He smiled at the thought. "Sent him to snatch some old lady's purse."

Without a word, Jacques pulled out an engraved silver money-clip and peeled off a bill to hand Wouter. Then he slid into the front seat beside Sprug who grinned at his boss. "Maybe we put some sweat on the kid?"

The jeep roared off. And Wouter crammed the twenty-guilder note down into his pocket as he watched it go.

#

When he reached the Rembrandtsplein again, Raj ran back into the hotel. Tim wasn't in the room.

Raj considered rereading the note for a clue. But there was no clue; he clearly remembered what the note said. And what was worse, he felt more and more certain that he understood what it meant.

As he turned to leave the room again he saw the Metro schedule on the lampstand. It had to be Tim's.

Raj headed north, across the Amstel. Along the Kloveniersburgwal and into the Walletjes. Past the old canal-front houses where brightly made-up women advertised their trade by sitting and waiting in the open bedroom windows.

He spent fifteen minutes dashing through the crowds on the Metro platform at Central Station. No Tim.

Raj stopped to look at a Metro map. There were stations all over the city! But there was one stop close to the hotel: Waterlooplein. If Tim had headed to the Metro, he'd have gone there, not to Central Station. It looked like a smaller station, maybe someone would remember seeing Tim.

Raj hurried out back to the street. He walked east along

the Oosterdok waterfront until he turned down Valkenburger-straat toward Waterlooplein. The thoroughfares were crammed with traffic and people. Raj knew Tim could be anywhere.

# # #

Tim stood in the metro station, on the street level at the top of the escalator leading down to the trains. He scanned the platform below, searching for a likely target. There she was! A smartly attired matron, clutching an assortment of shopping bags, stepped onto the "up" escalator. Her purse rested on the handrail.

He stepped quickly onto a descending treadboard and moved casually to the left balustrade. Fewer than ten inches of molding separated the two handrails. Tim was halfway there and closing fast. The purse still hung within easy reach.

He snatched it and bounded down the escalator as his suddenly screaming victim was carried up and away to the street. But her screams alerted a middle-aged man in a business suit who was just stepping onto the up escalator as Tim hit the bottom and began sprinting along the platform. Tim heard the man shout and take up the pursuit.

A train's doors slid shut and it glided away. There would be no escape by rail. Tim slowed his pace as he groped around in the purse. His pursuer began to gain on him. Tim's hand closed on the billfold and he frantically jerked it out. *Nothing! Nothing but credit cards!*

He flung the purse and the billfold aside in frustration. And he heard his pursuer stop to retrieve them. But Tim kept on running to the far end of the platform and another escalator which would take him back up to the street.

Doubled over with pain and exertion, Tim just stood and let the moving steps carry him up and away to safety. As he neared the top, he straightened up. And there stood Jacques at the top of stairs.

Tim spun around to plunge back down the escalator. But

there was Sprug, a dozen steps below him, blocking his escape. Tim turned slowly back to face Jacques.

CHAPTER 16

Jacques led the way and Sprug steered Tim to the jeep double-parked at the curb outside the station. When the burly ex-fighter roughly shoved Tim into the back seat, Jacques climbed in next to him holding a switchblade in his right hand which rested casually in his lap. Sprug hustled around the jeep and climbed in behind the wheel. Tires squealed and the jeep sped out into the traffic, along Valkenburgerstraat toward the waterfront.

"I was coming to see you, Jacques," Tim tried not to sound whiny. "I was gonna be there. I had the money."

"What was it? The police again, Tim?"

"No. These guys . . . they were after a big buy. Five thousand guilders."

"No canal to jump into? No escape?"

The jeep accelerated as Sprug swung it out and around a taxi pulling to the curb. Then Jacques and Tim jerked forward as Sprug hit the brakes for a traffic light.

# # #

Raj hurried across the street before the light changed. He would never have even seen the yellow jeep behind the red sports car, if he hadn't heard someone call his name. He turned just in time to see Tim double over behind the driver's seat as the thin man sitting beside him in the jeep slammed an elbow into his bruised rib cage.

"Timothy?" Raj hurried toward the vehicle where it waited in traffic. But just as he walked up beside the jeep, the light changed and the jeep leaped forward at the same instant that the man sitting next to Tim kicked the passenger door open and knocked Raj sprawling in the gutter.

Raj jumped to his feet and stood gasping for air as the jeep roared off, weaving in and out of traffic down the street. But when he saw the light in the next block turn to red, Raj began to sprint along the street next to the curb. If the light was a long one, he might make it.

He was still ten car lengths away when Tim looked back. But even at that distance Raj read the fear on his friend's face, and he knew those men were the ones Tim had been terrified would find him. The thin man looked back when Tim did. He said something to the driver and the jeep whipped out around the traffic, running along the tram tracks in the middle of the street and then made a sudden right turn against the light crossing in front of the waiting line of traffic.

Raj reached the corner just in time to see the jeep disappear into an alley a block away. He raced into the alley to see the jeep stopped 100 meters ahead, its way completely blocked by a garbage truck lifting a dumpster high overhead. He closed in on the run.

But suddenly the driver threw the jeep into reverse and Raj heard the engine whine as it shot backward right at him. He looked for a place to dodge. But the narrow alley was crammed tight between two buildings.

Just as suddenly as it had started back, the jeep stopped

again. And then jerked forward again, wheeled left, and bounced down a short pedestrian stairway to the bottom level of a three-story parking garage. Tires squealed again as the jeep raced back through the garage to the street.

By the time Raj reached the mouth of the alley, he just had time to see the jeep make a left turn three blocks to the east. He'd come so close. But it was gone. Tim was gone. And the fear Raj had felt for his young friend before was nothing compared to what he felt now.

He was looking around for a place to sit down and take off his modified brogans when he saw it. A flash of yellow through the trees. A block away. Through the park. On a parallel street. Speeding back to the west.

Raj yanked off the heavy boots and sprinted across the park, carrying them in his hand. He reached the westbound street just in time to see the jeep turn again, to the right and cross a bridge over the canal. There was still hope.

But before he reached the bridge a bell sounded. And the drawbridge began to creak upward to allow a small sailboat to pass. The jeep raced down the street along the far side of the canal and disappeared from sight.

# # #

Sprug followed the narrow canalside street for several blocks before he whipped around a corner, down a side street and pulled to a sudden halt. As he got out from behind the wheel and moved around the front of the vehicle, Tim saw his chance and vaulted over the side of the jeep, intent on sprinting back for the canal.

But he was too slow. Or Sprug was too quick. Because the big man landed a quick chop to the back of his neck, dazing Tim. Then the big man grabbed Tim under the arms and dragged him into the building, a deserted old auto-repair garage.

"Tie him down," Jacques ordered, rolling out a dusty

desk chair from a counter in the back of the garage. Sprug dumped Tim into the chair and began scrounging in the store-room for rope. By the time he'd returned and tied his last knot, Tim began to revive and moaned.

Sprug walked to the front door and checked the street. When he returned, he leaned against the front fender of a German sedan that had been stripped of its engine block. And he lit up a cigar to watch.

The first thing Tim saw in the dim light of the garage was Jacques' smiling face. He lurched against his bonds, but even his arms were lashed tight to the arms of the chair. He quit fighting.

"Jacques! I can make good. I'll go to Rembrandtsplein every night. I can do it! I'll make plenty of guilders for you."

"I'm sure you will, Tim. I never doubted it."

Tim watched as Jacques took a tiny packet of powder and sprinkled it carefully into a spoon. Then he flicked his engraved silver cigarette lighter and held the flame under the spoon until the powder melted and began to bubble around the edges.

When Jacques pulled the syringe out of his coat pocket, Tim once again saw Moira's face. And he tasted the bile rising with the fear in his own throat.

# # #

Raj, no longer winded by the time the bridge clanked back into place, dashed across the canal and tore down the street in the direction the jeep had disappeared. He'd slowed to a lope when he finally spotted the jeep down a sidestreet less than a block from the canal.

"Thanks God!" he whooped.

# # #

"You wanted a second chance, Tim? I will oblige you," Jacques said, pulling back the plunger to fill the syringe with heroin.

"The same chance you gave Moira?"

"Oh, no, Tim." Jacques turned to face him. But his smile was far from reassuring. "You are not about to die.

"More like a 'graduation.' You gain the honors without ever having to study."

He stepped to the side of Tim's chair and bent forward. "This will help you be more cooperative. You will need to see me every day. So Sprug won't have the worry of looking for you. It'll be good for our business . . . yours and mine . . ."

The door from the street banged open and Raj stepped into the twilight of the garage. "Timothy?"

A knife flashed in Sprugs' hand. And Jacques reached under his jacket and whipped out a German .38 automatic he'd had tucked under his belt at the small of his back.

Jacques instantly assessed the intruder. He was obviously not a narc. "Who in hell are you?" he asked.

Raj walked cautiously toward Tim. "I am far from hell, but I recognize you, sir. The Prince of Darkness is your master!"

Jacques laughed out loud.

Raj looked from Tim to Jacques and then to the slowly circling Sprug as he said, "You cannot have him."

"Big talk for a coolie!" Jacques said. Then to Tim: "Where did you find this fool?"

Tim's eyes remained fixed on Sprug. "He found me."

"And now the police will find him. In some alley with heroin swimming in his veins."

"Run, Raj! Get outta here!" Tim screamed.

Raj stood like a rock. "I do not go without you, Timothy."

Jacques nodded at Sprug who closed in waving his knife. "Then we make a little blood test."

Raj raised his hands, palms outward in front of his chest. "It is my wish to live peacefully with all men."

"Then you've come to the wrong place, mister," Jacques said. And Sprug charged.

Raj spun around and kicked in a blur. His bare heel drove like a hammer into Sprugs' throat, just above the breastbone. The man let out a shocked grunt and sagged to the floor, clutching at his throat and gasping for air. Jacques leveled the gun and fired, but the shot ricocheted wide as Tim lunged his chair sideways, rolling hard into the pusher and crashing over onto the floor. Jacques, his feet tangled under Tim, struggled to rise. Another lightning kick from Raj sent the gun flying across the garage, skittering under the engineless car where it dropped into the greasepit below.

Jacques dove for Sprug's knife. But Raj beat him to it and kicked the weapon away. Then he unleashed one more kick that snapped Jacques' head back and sent him crashing to the floor.

"Where'd the karate come from?" Tim asked as Raj righted his chair and began working on the ropes. "God teach you that in one of your little talks?"

Raj looked again at the two bodies slumped on the floor and tried to suppress a smile. "No," he said, shaking his head. "But I learned it from another very good teacher, my sergeant major. I spent two years in the service of my country.

"Come, Timothy," he said, hurriedly loosening the last of Tim's bonds. "They will wake soon. And the Lord knows I already have much to confess this day."

CHAPTER 17

Tim tried to concentrate on the scenery in order to control his increasing anxiety. And what he saw was picture-postcard Holland. Scattered windmills, like lonely sentinels, standing guard over the lush green landscape. And irrigation canals, the lifeblood of the land, crossing and criss-crossing fields stretching flat to the horizon.

Some of the small villages they passed through were little more than a cluster of farmhouses with fields radiating out around them. In the bright afternoon sunshine, windows glistened like polished gemstones set amid bright splashes of floral colors springing from window boxes and potted plants. Yards were trimmed. Front steps freshly swept. But the one word that best described the towns themselves was "immaculate," as if honored guests were expected at any moment.

Tim noted all this at the leisurely pace of a bicycle tourist. He had little to do besides sightseeing. Raj was doing all the pedaling. "Your ribs need the rest, Timothy," he had insisted. "At home, in India, many bicycles carry three passengers. One sits on seat, one rests on handlebars, and the driver pedals. This will not be hard. Besides, I can afford to rent only one bike for this afternoon."

He owed Raj for this. And for a lot more.

#

After their escape from Jacques and Sprug two days before, Raj had taken Tim back to the Schiller Hotel. But when he'd heard Tim's story and learned what Jacques had been planning and what had happened to Moira, Raj insisted that Tim go to the authorities.

"No way," Tim had responded. "I didn't escape from Jacques just to turn myself into the police and give up all my chances of going home."

"The man needs to be brought to justice. He murdered that woman, Timothy."

"But why should I have to pay to be the one who turns him in?" Tim asked.

Raj was silent for a time before he said, "Because if he gets away with this, he will do to someone else what he's done with you. And someday he will kill another person." He paused before he added, "But there is only one real reason you must go to the police, Timothy. You must do it because it is the right thing to do."

In the end, it was those words that convinced Tim: Because it is the right thing to do. After everything he'd done in the past few weeks, the thought of doing something he knew was right held surprising appeal. And the moment he told Raj he'd go to the police was the first time he'd felt good, really good, about himself since he'd left home.

Raj went with him to the police station. And an hour after an officer took Tim's statement about Moira, Jacques and Sprug were hauled into the station. Moira's body had been found the day before and termed a suicide. But with Tim's statement the case was reclassified as murder.

The moment Sprug was charged, he'd begun to talk. Or perhaps "croak" was a more accurate description of how he'd be communicating until his bruised larynx healed. Hoping to better his own situation, he told the police all about Jacques' network of drug dealing and prostitution. It seemed Jacques had been instrumental in a couple other recent "suicides." By the time Sprug finished his initial statement, the authorities had enough to build such a strong case against Jacques they hardly needed any other testimony. There would be no charges against Tim. He was a free man.

After that, Tim could hardly refuse when Raj insisted on taking him to meet the Peter Di Bie who lived at the address provided by the Manager-General of the VVV office. There was little chance of mistaken identity. How many Peter Di Bies could there be who returned from the United States in 1968 with degrees from San Francisco State University?

# # #

An hour and a half after they'd set out, Raj and Tim finally reached their destination, fifteen or sixteen miles south-southwest of Amsterdam. The village looked a little bigger than some they'd come through—population a thousand or so.

Raj pulled the bike to a stop at the curb in front of a small grocery and waited, straddling the bike, as Tim climbed off and went inside to ask directions. A minute later Tim exited, accompanied by a shopkeeper struggling to give directions in a mixture of Dutch and English. Mostly Dutch.

The man pointed down the street and held up four fingers. Then held up his hand to indicate a stop and pointed to the left. Tim shook his hand and thanked him before climbing back on the bike.

"This is the village?" Raj asked as he peddled away.

"He knows a Dr. Di Bie. Seems he's a veterinarian," Tim replied.

Raj gave an exuberant grin and began pumping harder.

Tim remained quiet until they reached the fourth block and turned left, when he said, "At least let me walk when we get there. Okay, Raj?"

"Just refer to me as your driver."

"Right."

The old cobblestone street made for a bumpy ride up and over a bridge spanning a small canal at the edge of town. Raj rolled to a stop at the next mailbox wih white lettering: "Di Bie." Raj waited at the road, smiling happily, as Tim took his first hesitant steps toward the substantial, red brick house, set well back off the street. The roof and corner of a barn could be seen beyond the house.

Tim turned and looked back at Raj. "What can I say to him?"

"The truth, brother."

"Sure. 'Hi there! By the way, we're related.'"

"Go on, Timothy."

"Aren't you coming?"

"California to Holland accompanied by India? It could give him a headache."

Tim forced a smile. "Hope he's had a good day so far . . ." And he walked toward the house.

The polished brass nameplate beside the door read "P. Di Bie, Dieren' Arts." Tim rang the bell. A few moments later he heard footsteps approaching the door. It seemed a wonder he could hear anything above the pounding of his heart.

A woman opened the door. She looked to be in her mid-thirties. Trim, dark hair. She looked quite proper, almost formal, despite an apron. "Goede middag. Kan ik je hepen?"

"I'm American. Sorry. I don't speak . . ."

"Yes? What is it?" she switched instantly to English.

Tim stood mute for a few seconds, trying to imagine his own mother standing there. Everything would have been so different, so . . .

"What is it you want?" The voice was not his mother's.

"I would like to meet . . . to see Mr. Di Bie."

"I am Mrs. Di Bie. Is this for an appointment? The doctor is quite busy. Are you selling something?"

"No . . . we've biked out from Amsterdam."

Mrs. Di Bie looked past Tim, toward the mailbox where Raj stood beside the bike. Raj waved and called, "The young man brings greetings from a friend in America."

She looked back to Tim, puzzlement in her expression.

"I was about to say that," Tim added quickly.

"The doctor is in the barn. You may go around," she said. And as Tim descended the steps and started around the house, she quickly closed the door and moved to the living room window to watch him go.

Tim stopped for almost a full minute outside the barn, taking several deep breaths and trying to collect both his thoughts and his courage. Then he nudged open the side door and stepped inside.

As with most old barns, considerable daylight filtered in through cracks between slightly warped and weatherbeaten boards. But the openings to the outside air did little to diffuse the smell of hay and animals.

Along one whole side of the barn stood a long row of curious cages and pens that reminded Tim of something out of his old children's stories about Dr. Doolittle, or perhaps of James Herriot. One pen contained a spotted goat nursing twin kids, one of which had a splinted leg. There was a German shepherd with a bandaged eye and his head sticking out of a ridiculous bucketlike contraption evidently rigged to keep him from scratching at his wound. Smaller cages held an assortment of rabbits, cats, and a bright green parrot. The dog barked and all the animals stirred restlessly as Tim walked through the barn.

At the far end of the building Tim saw a man with his back turned, bent over and examining the left-front fetlock of a chestnut mare.

"Hello," Tim called. "Is Dr. Di Bie here?"

The man stood slowly, ran his hand under the horse's muzzle, and finally turned around. "Yes? Good afternoon."

A little boy lies in bed, staring at the picture on the night-stand, knowing he won't be going to the Cub Scout father-son night. He decides he won't even mention it to his mom. No sense making her think she has to find a friend to go with him.

# # #

His mom sits on the edge of his bed crying. The picture smashes into the wall. The frame cracks and glass shatters to the floor.

The face was older. But the years of careful study had etched the lines of the forehead, the nose, the eyes into his memory. Tim had said so much to that face. Crying out his loneliness in childhood. Talking out his plans, his dreams. But the sight of his father standing in front of him now, in this place, struck him silent.

The doctor moved to another stall. "You will have to come to me. I'm running late this afternoon."

Tim stepped forward, closing the distance between them, as his father looked at him again. "Do I know you? Have we met?"

Rustling animal sounds filled the barn.

"Not exactly," Tim managed to reply.

"Then please state your business. My schedule rules me today."

Tim pulled out his wallet and extracted the folded page of the yearbook. "Sir, I just wanted to bring you this."

The vet stepped out of the stall and reached for the paper. "Has somebody decided to sue me? I would not take you for a prosperous lawyer. But then, perhaps you are incognito?" He smiled at Tim and then began to unfold the paper and stare at the two circled pictures.

Tim watched his father's face. The man was obviously

baffled.

"But where did you find such a thing?"

The answer to that question had seemed so easy when he had rehearsed it in his mind. He'd imagined his response a thousand times, choosing and rechoosing the words, the inflection of voice. And now, none of those words would come.

Tim swallowed. "Janet Dirksen is my mother . . ." His voice choked with emotion. "And she informed me . . . somewhat reluctantly . . . that I am your son."

Now that Tim had found the words, the doctor seemed to have lost all his. He stared, open-mouthed, as Tim continued.

"You lived together in San Francisco in 1967-1968. I was born a few months after you returned to The Netherlands."

The big door of the barn swung open and sunlight poured in behind a teen-age boy, thirteen or fourteen years old, pushing a wheelbarrow piled with bags of feed. The boy said something in Dutch.

Tim understood only the word "Vader"—Father. He turned to look at the boy, his own half-brother, then back at the still silent doctor. "Well, anyway . . . you've got the pictures. And I'm tired of carrying them around." With that, he rushed past the boy and out into the blinding sunlight.

"Wait!" The doctor found his voice. "What do I call you?"

"You don't!" Tim called back without breaking his stride.

#

"What happened?" Raj asked when Tim reached the road.

"Nothing," Tim snapped. "Let's just get out of here. It was stupid to let you drag me out here. And it was even stupider to come to this country in the first place." He swung his leg over the bike.

But Raj didn't budge. "Did you expect him to invite you to tea after such news?"

"How do I know what I expected? Or did God tell you that, too?"

Raj put his hand on Tim's arm. "I feel it is too fast, Timothy. Perhaps he needs time . . ."

"*He* needs time? Sure! Great! How about another eighteen years of my life? After all, we've only got a slight misunderstanding here!"

"I'll go back with you. We'll talk to him."

Tim jerked his arm away angrily and climbed off the far side of the bike, knocking it to the ground in the process. "You're out of it now, Raj! Okay?" Before Raj could say anything, Tim went on. "You think I don't know your game? You're just set on claiming me for Jesus. And for your God squad back at the Rai Center." Raj started to reply but was cut off before he got a word out. "Well, forget it, chief! Forget about me. I'll live my own life without any more help from you!"

Raj stood and watched as Tim took off running down the road, over the little bridge, and back toward the middle of town. He stooped to pick up the fallen bike and then as he climbed on, he saw Dr. Di Bie, walking from the barn. The doctor glanced around, hurrying toward the road, obviously looking for Tim.

So Raj coasted into the drive to meet the veterinarian.

CHAPTER 18

D arkness finally descended over the Dutch countryside nearly three hours after Raj headed back to Amsterdam alone. From a vantage point in a small stand of trees some distance from the road, Tim had watched the Indian pedaling north. Raj had hung around the town for a time, asking questions, trying to find someone who'd seen a young American on foot. But he'd had to get back to Amsterdam and return the rented bike before dark.

Once Raj had gone, Tim hurried back through town and found another secluded spot to sit and wait amid some bushes lining the little canal at the edge of the village. From there he had a clear view of the red brick house and the barn behind it.

One after another, lights came on in the windows around the house. And with the night shadows, Tim crept from his hiding spot, toward the house.

In keeping with Dutch custom, the curtains remained open. So as Tim edged up to peer in the large living room window in the front of the house, he could see the family sitting in the dining room enjoying their late evening meal. Mrs. Di Bie sat with her back to the window, her husband directly opposite her across a heavy, square oak table. The boy from the barn sat on the right; Tim wished he knew his name. And on the left was a beautiful little six-year-old girl with long blonde hair. *A sister.*

Tim couldn't hear what was being said. But the boy seemed to be doing most of the talking. And the little girl laughed and responded from time to time. As he watched the family through the window, he couldn't help but think of the quiet suppers he and his mom had often shared as they sat on the barstools of their kitchen breakfast counter.

Perhaps it was only Tim's imagination, but the doctor's expression seemed pensive, almost distracted throughout the meal. And as Mrs. Di Bie stood and began clearing the table, he walked toward Tim, through the living room to the front door.

Tim ducked into the shadows around the side of the house as the front door opened and closed again. And when he poked his head out to see around the corner, there stood the doctor on the front stoop, cupping his hand to light his pipe and then settling down on the steps in the cool evening air.

Standing like a statue, Tim watched the dark silhouette of his father sitting fewer than ten feet away. He felt sure he knew what the man was thinking about. He only wished he could read those thoughts.

After a time the front door opened once more and the little girl came out to throw her arms around her father's neck in a giant hug and say, "Welterusten, Vader." Her father pulled her playfully over his shoulder and tickled her in his lap until she was giggling with pleasure and squealing, "Nee, Pa, nee!" Then he stood, hoisted the still giggling girl over his shoulder and carried her inside to bed.

Five minutes later Tim headed for the road and began the long trek back to Amsterdam.

#

Midnight.

The only light in the hotel room came from the flashing neon lights of the Rembrandtsplein outside the window. Abraham had gone to the room of some African friends to fellowship and talk on this last evening before the conference ended.

Raj felt grateful to be alone for a while. He sat in the darkness on the bed, Tim's guitar resting across his lap, trying to pick out the chords for "Homeland on the Range." The tune bore even less of a resemblance to the original than did his words. To call his musicianship poor would have been overly gracious. But even as he strummed and sang, Raj's thoughts were miles away in the night. He finally went to sleep, but he tossed uneasily until morning.

#

Tim knocked a second time on the door of Room 412. Still nothing. The clock in the lobby had said it was 9:08. Maybe he was too late. Slowly he walked back down the hall, turning to look at the closed door one more time before he stepped into the waiting and open elevator.

Back in the lobby, Tim walked to the reception desk. "Could you tell me, please, has Mr. Prasad checked out of Room 412?"

The clerk checked his computer and then shuffled through a small stack of cards in front of him. "I do not show his departure, but there has been much confusion. Many conference participants did leave this morning and will be going to the airport from the Rai Center later today."

"Thanks," Tim replied as he started across the lobby to the door. Maybe he wasn't too late.

#

Billy Graham stood behind the pulpit, concluding the conference with his final address to the delegates filling the

Europahal.

"What if you knew Christ would return in one minute and you were the only person in the world who knew it? Would you fall on your knees and cry out for mercy, realizing you've never really known him?

"Suppose you were the only one to know Christ would return in thirty seconds. Would you run out into the street and scream at the top of your voice, 'Jesus is coming! Repent and believe! Repent and believe'?"

The loud speakers amplified his voice through the auditorium. The giant projection screen above the platform magnified his face so that everyone in the hall could read his expression, his every gesture.

"Suppose there were twenty seconds and you realized you'd not lived a holy life, you're not ready to see Jesus, and you're now desperate. Ten seconds . . . Nine . . . Eight . . . Seven . . . Five . . . Four . . . Two . . . One. And you're not ready.

"God has entrusted to people like you and me, redeemed sinners, the responsibility of carrying out his divine purpose. He has given us the privilege, the high and holy privilege to proclaim his message of the Gospel of the Kingdom. Let us therefore ask God to give us a fresh vision of the world outside Christ. A world for which Christ died. A world which is filled with fear, chaos and spiritual emptiness.

"How many of us have loved people for Christ so much that we've shed tears?" Abraham turned and met Raj's eye as Dr. Graham continued. "Do you see people every day? Do you look at them as lost people, separated from God, with empty hearts, searching for something—something they don't know . . . is God.

"I do not believe any of us is here by chance. God has brought each of us here for a purpose. And may each of us go from Amsterdam with a new commitment to do the work of an evangelist."

He paused, looking around the great assembly. "There is just one word that all of us can say in every language. Let's say it together! Hallelujah!"

The crowd echoed back.

"Hallelujah!"

And the crowd shouted it louder.

"Hallelujah!" he shouted.

And the building fairly rattled with the final response: "HALLELUJAH!"

"Now," said Billy Graham as the echoes of that thunderous shout faded away, "go out and do the work of an evangelist."

A scattering of "Amen's" rose from the crowd.

"Do the work of an evangelist!"

More "amen's."

"Do the work of an evangelist!"

Thunder again as 8,000 voices raised as one to shout, "Amen."

"Now unto him who is able to keep you from falling, and to present you faultless before the presence of his glory with exceeding joy, to the only wise God, our Savior, we give the power, the glory, the majesty, and the dominion, both now and ever more. Amen."

The "Amen" thunder rolled once more. And the historic conference was over.

# # #

Participants streamed out of the Rai Center, across the walks to a seemingly endless row of buses lining the street. Multicolored clusters of people gathered everywhere, shaking hands, embracing new friends, sharing bittersweet goodbyes. Raj and Abraham stood alone, facing each other a few feet outside the Rai Center doors.

The older African smiled and hugged Raj. "God keep you, son."

"And you," Raj replied, emotion filling his chest and throat.

Abraham looked toward the line of buses and shook his head. "Ah, the West!" he grinned at his young friend. Raj managed a smile as Abraham's tone turned more serious. "Such strong meat . . . our days here. Need sit alone . . ." He patted between his stomach and his heart. ". . . to take in."

He placed his hand on Raj's shoulder and nodded. "We not meet again until . . ." He pointed to the sky and grinned.

Raj nodded silently, not trusting himself to speak. Instead he offered his hand. Abraham clasped it firmly and said, "I will pray for Timothy."

Then Raj hugged Abraham once more before the African stooped to pick up his suitcase and headed for the curb. Raj watched his friend climb aboard a bus before he turned and walked down the sidewalk away from all the friendly and emotional leave-taking.

But less than a block from the Rai Center he glanced across the street and instantly froze. There at a bus stop, leaning casually against a kiosk, stood Tim. The moment Raj spotted him, Tim raised his hand, the one carrying his sleeveless denim jacket, in a minimal gesture of greeting.

Raj whooped and zigzagged through the traffic to the other side of the street.

"Hiya, chief!" Tim grinned. "I was afraid I'd missed you. And I didn't figure you should take off for home without some kind of a goodbye."

"Many are leaving today. But my flight is not until tomorrow." He pumped Tim's hand enthusiastically. "Timothy . . . thank you."

"Well, you know, suppose I decided later on to shift to your side? It'd be a huge hassle to look you up in India. From what I hear, it's a pretty big place."

Raj looked puzzled. "'Shift to your side'? This expression is not known to me."

"Well, you said the only sure way was to *try* him. And that he's as real to you as any living person. So I'm thinking about making a sort of test for myself. To see whether or not you're . . ." He gestured in a circle with his index finger next to his ear.

As Raj recognized the sign language for "madness," he grinned in understanding and excitement. "Timothy! You are asking to be a Christian?" He poised like a Bengal tiger about to spring.

Tim held up both hands and stepped back. "Hey, I'm feeling my way through this. Okay?" He'd had all night to think. To replay everything that had happened since he'd arrived in Amsterdam. And he hadn't been able to get Raj's words out of his mind.

When Tim turned and began sauntering along the walk, Raj hurried up beside him, to walk silently at his side. He didn't want to push. Not now. So a block passed before Tim broke the silence.

"I've got a lot of garbage in my life to dump first."

"You have no need to worry. He is like a lowly street-sweeper in my country. He will take it all away for you." And he began to quote 1 John 1:9—"'If we confess our sins to him, he can be depended upon to forgive us and to cleanse us from every wrong.' And then you must ask him to be Lord of your life."

They paused at a street corner waiting for the light to change. "But I don't know what that means."

"He will show you," Raj said.

How can Raj be so sure? His faith seemed so simple, so naïve. And yet Tim knew Raj wasn't asking him to take any real risk. *Just try him,* he'd said. It was so simple. So hard.

They stopped walking at the middle of a bridge. Tim leaned against the rail, looking down to the still, green water of the canal. "I don't know how to do this," he said.

"You can start by talking to Jesus," Raj said. "The words

do not really matter. He understands your heart."

Tim stared at the water. Finally he began to pray softly. "Raj says You already know about me, Jesus. So there's not much point in repeating myself. I've hurt a lot of people . . . including myself. I know that. . . . I'm sorry. Please make it right. I want to believe in You." He glanced over at Raj who had his eyes closed. "I guess I'm opening the door."

Tim fell silent. Waiting. For something. He didn't know what he'd expected. A voice? Bright lights? An overpowering feeling that would convince him for all eternity that he'd just made the most important decision of his life?

None of that happened. Nothing happened. Or almost nothing. It wasn't really a feeling. More like a quiet calmness after the passing of a storm.

Tim stood up slowly. And when Raj opened his eyes, Tim smiled at him. "Is that it? I expected something more. Some feeling . . ."

"Everyone's feelings are different," Raj said. "But the fact of God's forgiveness is always the same."

He wanted to believe that. He did believe that. It wasn't so much a feeling as it was a knowing. Raj had been right. And now he was right. After so much wrong, he was right now. Somehow he knew it. And the knowing felt good. Tim nodded and then smiled his assurance at Raj.

Raj's face split into a grin. "My heart is singing! I can barely hold it in place." Indeed, he practically skipped all the way back to the hotel.

# # #

Raj paced up and down the sidewalk in front of the Schiller Hotel, carefully studying each passing car. Finally a gray sedan slowed and pulled to the curb. Behind the wheel sat Peter Di Bie.

Raj rushed to the driver's window to greet him. "Thanks God. He's waiting inside for us . . . I hope." He shrugged.

"Timothy . . . is Timothy."

Tim spotted them the moment they walked into the lobby. He rose slowly from the couch where he'd been sitting and approached.

His father spoke first. "Hello, Tim."

"Hi," he responded. The awkwardness stretched between them like a bottomless gorge.

Raj stepped into the gap for a moment and smiled at Tim, then at Tim's father. "I must leave you alone for a while. I am late for a meeting with the hotel operator. We have become very good friends." And he was gone.

The two of them stood silent for a few seconds until Tim's father indicated two nearby chairs. "Shall we sit?"

"Sure, why not?" *How do you start your first meaningful conversation with your father after eighteen years? Of all the things to say, where do you begin? You have to start somewhere.* And that's what Tim did.

Father and son were still talking when Raj stepped back into the lobby to check on them an hour later.

CHAPTER 19

Tim stood at a pay phone in a busy corridor in the terminal at Schiphol International Airport. Across the hall, leaning against a canteen counter and stirring a cup of coffee, Peter Di Bie waited and watched his son.

Tim pressed a finger into the ear away from the phone as he tried to hear the words from the other end of the call. Finally he responded, "Don't worry, Mom. I'll clear customs in New York. It won't take any time at LAX." He turned away, toward the wall, and lowered his voice, "He really does want to talk to you. Yeah! He's waiting . . . okay? Just a minute . . . what? Love you too."

He left the receiver dangling gently by the cord and quickly crossed the corridor. "Mom . . . uh, she really wants to talk to *you!*"

Peter Di Bie looked over at the phone and then at Tim and nodded. He crossed, picked up the receiver, and smiled back at Tim before he said, "Hello? Janet?" He listened a few seconds and winked at Tim as he said, "Tell me, do you still like to eat ice cream for breakfast?" Tim grinned. "Of course, I haven't forgotten. Even after twenty years, some things, some people stay in your . . ."

Tim turned toward a commotion coming down the corridor. Raj, clamped by the elbows between two security guards, was calling, "Timothy! There he is! I told you he was waiting here. You see."

The guards released their grips and Raj hurried ahead of them toward Tim, holding out the guitar case. Tim glanced over at the bank of phones where his father was still talking, oblivious to the ruckus.

"Your guitar, Timothy," Raj said, offering the instrument. "You left it at the hotel. I explained to these gentlemen that it would be a great loss to you. But since I did not have a ticket to show at the security gate, they wished to accompany me here." He turned to the guards. "Timothy is a musician, most professional."

"It's yours, Raj," Tim pushed the guitar away. "I want you to have it."

"But . . . Really? . . . You do?"

He dropped his voice to a whisper. "But they suspect I am a smuggler. You are required to take it."

"There has been a misunderstanding," Tim announced to the guards. "I gave him the guitar."

Raj looked from one guard to the other. "Do you want to look inside again?" He offered the case.

"No. But we must go." As the guards closed in on Raj again, Tim held up his hand asking them to wait a moment.

"Guess we should finish this off right, huh?"

Raj grinned and handed his guitar to the nearest guard and locked Tim in a giant bear hug, nearly lifting him off his feet. "If you think I have troubles here, wait until they see my beautiful guitar in New Delhi. At least I have thirteen hours to work out a good story."

Tim laughed, even as his eyes misted up. "Wish I could

be there to hear it." And as the Indian backed slowly away, Tim added, his voice choked with emotion, "Thanks, Raj . . . for being my friend."

The guards were ushering Raj away as he called back over his shoulder, "God go with you, Timothy."

# # #

Boarding pass in hand, Tim stood in the line at the departure gate. Peter Di Bie, with Tim's backpack slung over one shoulder, stood beside him.

"If it's . . . uh . . . okay," Tim said, "I'd like to . . . write you."

"Do!" his father said. "And maybe we could plan on you coming for another visit next summer."

"I'd like that."

The line began to move. Peter Di Bie reached out to shake Tim's hand. Then he pulled him into a quick embrace. When he released him, he slipped the pack from his own shoulder to Tim's.

"Thanks again for . . ." Tim raised his boarding pass and then turned to walk out the jetway. And the way he felt at that moment, he doubted he even needed a plane to soar across the Atlantic.

# # #

When his plane rolled into the blocks alongside the terminal with the familiar space-age arches of LAX, Tim had to fight the urge not to push his way to the door. He did pass several passengers in the jetway in his rush out into the waiting area. *They aren't here.*

He jogged down the concourse, following the signs to the baggage claim area, but always scanning the faces ahead. He was halfway down the escalator to the lower level when he heard Aimee's scream. "Tim!"

Then he saw them, across the stairs, on the up escalator.

Aimee squealing and waving. His mom beside her, flashing a grin. They reached the top before he got to the bottom and Aimee dashed down the stairs. She fairly leaped into his arms from the bottom step and he swung her around in the air as she laughed and cried in his ear.

When he finally set her down, she gave him her most practiced look of displeasure and scanned him from head to toe. "Tim!" she shrieked again. "Where are your boots?"

He looked down at Raj's sandals and smiled. "Later," he said. "It's a very long story."

He turned and bounded up the stairs to his mom, stopping on the step below her, their eyes on a level. She put her arms on his shoulders and clasped him behind the neck. "Sorry we didn't get here before now. Your plane must have been early."

Tim stood looking into his mother's eyes for a time before he replied, "No, Mom, I'm the one who is late." And as the tears began trickling down his face, he pulled her to him and laid his head on her shoulder. "Real late."

# # #

In the crowded marketplace of a tiny village in north central India, Rajam Prasad sat on the back of an ox cart piled with ripe melons. On his lap he held a guitar. And he sang an Indian hymn.

Those who might have been put off by the sound of his playing, were instead attracted by the openness and warmth reflected in his smile. A crowd quickly gathered. Children crouched on the ground by his feet. Adults pressed in to listen as he began to talk.

"I will tell you today a great love story. Greater than any you have ever heard. It was born in the heart of God who gave us life! His love was so great that he sent his Son to walk the earth with us and to die so we could know the light of heaven. His Son came to our darkness from a land brighter than our summer sky . . ."

#

Tim Devon sat in the sand, holding Aimee's hand and looking out over the great Pacific toward India. That's where he told her about Raj and his 8,000 friends who had been in Amsterdam and now had scattered around the world. How it warmed him to think of all those people out there, in the deep pockets of world, giving people the same challenge Raj had given him. To make his own test of God.

And there, under the brightness of a California summer sky, he told Aimee about the decision he made in Amsterdam. Not the easiest decision he had ever made. Only the best.